A WOMAN'S STORY.

BY

MRS. S. C. HALL.

"—— those first affections,
Those shadowy recollections,
Which, be they what they may,
Are yet the fountain light of all our day."
WORDSWORTH.

IN THREE VOLUMES.
VOL. II.

LONDON:
HURST AND BLACKETT, PUBLISHERS,
SUCCESSORS TO HENRY COLBURN,
13, GREAT MARLBOROUGH STREET.
1857.
The right of Translation is reserved.

A WOMAN'S STORY.

CHAPTER I.

"Yet here high passions, high desires unfold,
Prompting to noblest deeds."

ROGERS.

"WELL!" exclaimed little Major Cobb, after
three ineffectual attempts to obtain for his
hand a comfortable resting-place on the window
of the high built carriage, which, through doing
duty for a number of years as 'glass-coach' at
Hampstead, would have 'cut up' into I know
not how many 'broughams,' or double-bodied
'flies;' "well, really, well," he repeated, having
gained his breath, ' you *are* moving! why you

must be a fortune to the job-master; and
they do say, you had a coach waiting for you
on the hill the other night, and all day
yesterday—a glass-coach, and another to day !
It doesn't do you good, indeed it does not,
for all that," persisted the little Major, rolling
up his eyes to me, " it does not do you good ;
you look as if just off a forced march—great
fatigue, and short rations. Mrs. Cobb (she's
sadly off her limbs, poor soul —can't outwalk
me), Mrs. Cobb wants to know—indeed, when
Tozer said the yellow coach was again at your
door this morning—Mrs. Cobb sent me to
ask," and he stood on the the tops of his toes,
while I bent my head out of the window to hear
what it was he wished to inquire about, *sotto
voce*, " Mrs. Cobb wants to know if Green, the
job-master, charges you three-and-sixpence the
first hour, and three shillings every hour afterwards, when you have the carriage so frequently ? She says, if he does, it is a shame,
and you ought not to submit to it. They are
all great rogues, and if you go on paying full
price, when you have the carriage so often,
why he will expect us all to do the same thing,
and there will be no end to the expense."

I was obliged to say I feared I had not been as provident in this matter as became me, and confessed that, in one way or other, I paid Green a considerable income.

"It would have been better for you to have been neighbourly with the Saunders', and joined them in a carriage all the year round, day about to use it, and every second Sunday; so Mrs. Cobb says."

"And the Saunders, say, Major," I replied, not, I confess, with my usual prudence, "that the best way of all would be for you to lend them your carriage occasionally to take a drive in—better than keeping it in the huge coach-house as a nesting-place for sparrows. As to me, I like to be mistress of my own actions: and, perhaps, the day I wanted the carriage would be the very day I could not have it."

"Indeed," replied the good-natured little man, "indeed, what you say about the carriage is very true, but Mrs. Cobb does not like the family arms, after all the trouble she had to find them, to go about without her." Again he rolled his round eyes up to me. "It's true

enough what Mrs. Brevet says—she says, ' I
tell you what, Cobb, our NOBODY is beginning
to cut up uncommon sharp—always in march-
ing order.' But take my hint of the three-
and-sixpence for the first, and three shillings
for the second hour. Why, there isn't a man
in England who would not be shot at for half
the sum per day; just think of that !"

" I must bid you good morning, Major. I
have an early appointment."

" Ay, we know, we know !" he answered;
" we all know—you fancy you can move about
just as you like."

" Indeed," I replied, with as much earnestness as truth, " I do not; I never fancied such
a thing; and if I had, the good people of
Hampstead would have undeceived me."

" Ay, but we don't mind you a bit; and I
say to Mrs. Cobb, if our friend at the Dove-
cote tells us nothing, she tells nothing of us."

Alas! if the poor Major were alive, I wonder what he would say of me now! I called
at Mrs. Middleton's, and found that Florence
and Mrs. Dellamere had gone out, and that
Mr. Middleton had not returned. I felt very

confused at the stage-door of the Theatre
Royal, but my self-possession did not desert
me, and I presented my note at the dingy entrance, to a man who sat inside a very dark-
boarded lodge, and who stared at me from
behind a counter, upon which he had just
rested a pot of porter, and a very long pipe.

"The manager is gone home an hour ago,"
said the official, looking as straight in my face
as if he were telling the truth, "he went
home an hour ago, and won't be here until to-
morrow morning; he does not act to-night."

"You are mistaken," I replied, "the manager is here at this moment, and you must take
him this note. He is about to read a play
which I am to hear."

He first of all fixed his eyes on me;—
then, looking carefully round the room, and
up at a bill of the night's performance, as if
anxious to ascertain that every moveable was
secure from being carried off, he placed an
empty can with the greatest tenderness over
the full one, so as to risk as little injury as possible to the frothy head, then called "Bill," (an
in-toed, cranky looking bull-terrier, whose phy-

siognomy was not improved by one eye being
black and a cut over the other) and sprang
over what I thought was a counter, but which
was only a very peculiar table. " Mind the
office, Bill," he said, and Bill answered " Yes,"
with a movement of his stumpy tail. The
porter then went to the door for the purpose of
inspecting the conveyance in which I came.
The result, I suppose, was satisfactory, for he
touched his hat as he passed, and Bill, understanding the civility, made another movement
of his tail to me, and in an astonishingly good-
natured way, advanced to the edge of the
table, and placed his foot on my glove, looking
into my face with a species of canine confidence, which, in a bull-terrier, bordered upon
vulgar familiarity, in a spaniel or greyhound
the same movement would have been the perfection of elegance. I love dogs, I do not
mean to say as some ladies say of children,
' I like them *in their proper places;*' I say I
love them; I love them everywhere except in my
lap. I delight in seeing the graceful bound
of my greyhounds over the Heath, spring after
spring, with their necks arched, their trans-

parent ears erect, their tails slightly curled, in earnest chase after a rabbit or a bird; I like to hear their short, provoked bark, when they flush a lark, which, after a moment or two, sings on poised wings above their heads. How full of beautiful and energetic life they are! and I love almost as well the fearless plunge of the noble Newfoundland dog into the waters which close round, without bending his brave head. I enjoy more than even the sportsman, the sagacity of the setter, and have a world of friendship for our old rat-catchers' keen-nosed dogs—things as remarkable for intelligence as they are for ugliness; steady-going creatures, that look neither to the right nor the left, but move on in a line after their old master's heels, reversing the usual order of precedence, the youngest going first, and the grandfather bringing up the rear; they never notice anything on the road, except a hole by the wayside, at which they stop and sniff, until they reach the field of their labours, and then nothing escapes them, rat or mouse. It seems always matter of inquiry of their master, whether or not the cat of the household

where their services are required is to be
considered 'vermin;' the animal, aware of
this, always sets them at defiance, and places
herself on some tower of strength, out of
their reach.   The little long-bodied sky-
terrier, muffy and hedgehoggy as it is, ill-
tempered and 'snarly' to its acquaintances,
but staunch and loving to its friends, has
a large portion of my regard; while the
timid, shy little spaniel—a very dove among
dogs—unchanging, unmoving, but in my foot-
steps, has a mine of tenderness in its moist
round eyes, a world of gratitude and patience
circling about its heart.   I should be ungrate-
ful indeed if I did not regard the whole canine
race as friends, for the sake of that one little
spaniel.   Even this ugly play-house dog, who
was certainly fitted neither for a tragic nor a
comic part, and was too low almost for farce—
this poor brute seemed perfectly to understand
that I had a friendly feeling towards all his
race.   His under jaw stuck out considerably
below the upper, and was garnished by a
cheveux de frise of teeth that were anything
but friendly in their aspect; still he leered at

me with such subdued feeling, that I returned his civility by patting his head, upon which a soiled, though not a dirty girl, whom I had not before observed, issued from behind a sort of screen that protected the fire from the wind of the door, and exclaimed—

"Take care, ma'am; no one touches 'Bill' but the porter; he is not friends with me; do, lady, take care, take care." But there was no danger. I patted Bill, and when the girl came near him he put up the bristles of his back—a sufficient warning to her, who knew his ways.

"Do you live here, child?" I said to the pale, intelligent-looking creature, who seemed covered by remnants of finery—not clothes—and had withal so suffering, yet so patient a face, that it long remained with me.

"About. I clean the office and the passage a little, and bring the gentleman here his dinner; and of a night I sell playbills, and in a little time I may be able to have a basket of oranges and get to the gallery with them. We shall do very well then."

"Have you a mother?"

"I do not think she is alive, lady; she was always so fond of us, she would not have left us."

"How many sisters have you?"

"Three, lady."

"Younger or older than you?"

"One older, two younger."

"And what does the eldest do?" The girl hung her head and made no reply, then looked up and said,—"The youngest of all goes on in the pantomimes and dances; she is a little beauty, indeed every one says so. The other helps me, but we both take great care of the little one."

I took out my purse, intending to season the good advice I gave with half-a-crown, but some idea of carefulness and the expense of glass coaches, palsied my charity. I gave her a longer lecture and only a shilling; still it seemed a great deal to her. She thanked me with both tears and smiles, and, hearing the porter's step, slunk behind the screen. The official's manner was quite changed. He begged my pardon—could not (he requested me to consider) know who I was—affected the greatest astonishment at 'Bill's' friendly advances—and, telling me not to be alarmed at the darkness, led the way to the greeen-room. We had not proceeded far, when I heard a step—the light step of youth—rapidly following :

"I beg your pardon, ma'am, but you have dropped your purse." It was the young girl from whom my little fit of parsimony had abstracted eighteen pence. I confess I was glad of the excuse to make peace with myself, and give her five shillings.

"Little Bess, I must say, is honest; I don't think she ever kept anything she found," said the man, "not even when they were worse off than they are now, when her father was in prison, and her mother, as we thought, dying. I've got a promise for her in the mobs and pantomimes, but she does not know it; it would elate her so much—a shilling a-night regular —it will be enough to elate her!" and he looked round at me during this pompous announcement of dramatic wealth.

"I think she has talent," he continued, in the spirit of self-gratulation which we all indulge in more or less, " and there's nothing so pleasant as bringing talent forward. Who knows but the time may come when she'll go on in speaking characters? I've seen stranger things than that in my time ; " and he threw open the door of a very handsome saloon, where a number of ladies and gentlemen were grouped round a table. I own I felt dizzy and confused. They all seemed so much more repectable and quiet than I had expected. I am ashamed to confess it now, but I had so strange an idea of the company I was going into, that I had absolutely left my watch on my dressing table, and though I had returned for it, lest I should not be to the minute with my appointment, I put it into my pocket, instead of passing the chain round my neck. The manager received me with the ease and kindness of a well-bred gentleman, and after calling over the names of some of those present, the company saluted me with exceeding courtesy, and I was placed on a sort of divan, next to a very lady-like person, and at the right hand of the manager, who placed the MS. on a desk before him.

"My reading, I fear, will weary you, you have so often heard it," he said to me.

"Indeed I have not; I have never heard or seen a line of it," I replied; "and I am very anxious to do so."

The manager smiled; and I saw the company look at each other, and then at me, rather more than was consistent with good breeding.

After a few observations, and an entreaty to one particular gentleman to keep quiet—he commenced reading first, the *dramatis personæ*, and then the dialogue. A moment before I had thought to myself how unlike this last and youngest, of our great dramatic family, was to the glorious creatures whose wonderful acting was an era in our history, and who are identified with some of the greatest characters therein. His features were certainly inferior to theirs in dignity, and his eloquent mouth had a degree of coarseness which marred the propriety (if I may so call it) of his face. This was the impression the first moments of our meeting left upon me; but when the pure and delicate declamation with which he read the early passages of the play deepened into

interest, and he entered into the spirit of the
scenes, I forgot where I was.   I only saw the
wonderful expression of his mobile face, while
my ears drank in with astonishment and delight the music of his varied voice.   What an
enjoyment it was!—the sound enriching the
sense—the keen appreciation of every sentiment and word of beauty rendering all more
beautiful.   The first act was little more than
introductory, and a judicious placing of the
characters in the interest of the audience—a
delicate shadowing forth of the purity and
difficulties of a passion which, if unsuccessful,
must terminate in the destruction of her, who
bade fair to rise from the woman into the
heroine.   This was simple enough; but it was
so arranged as to command and retain attention and sympathy; and when the reader said
—"So ends the first act," there was clapping
of hands, and the lady next to me, drawing
her breath heavily and falling back (she had
advanced and bent forward her head so as not
to lose a single word), simply murmured,
"Good, so far."

"I call it beautiful!" exclaimed a bright-

eyed, dark-haired, animated, and richly-en-
amelled woman, who had ceased pulling (in a
caressing manner) the ears of the beautiful
spaniel she held on her lap, after the first
few sentences. " I call it beautiful, which
is very disinterested, for a single line has not
yet been read that would suit me."

" Patience !" said the manager, holding up
his finger ; " you must wait until all is finished
before you determine. Patience."

The second act increased the interest ; the
third electrified us, and closed, so as to create
intense curiosity to learn how poetical justice
could be rendered. A running fire, of the
most keen satire, relieved, without disturbing the more serious interest of the drama ;
and repartee followed repartee as rapid and
brilliant as flashes of lightning.

CHAPTER II.

"Into the troubled ocean of that life,
Where all is turbulence, and toil, and strife."
BOWLES.

———

"AND now," said the manager, as he closed
the last blotted leaf of the MS., "I hope,
ladies and gentlemen, you are convinced that
in no respect have I overrated the merits of
this extraordinary play—combining, as it does,
intense interest and pathos, with brilliant wit,
a freedom and freshness of composition, with
the most elaborate knowledge of the drama's
rules. There are one or two somewhat ques-
tionable situations, but they do not change my
faith in the effect of the whole; and I am

sure you will unite with me in congratulating
this lady upon the anticipated, indeed I may
say, the certain, success of the play."

I suppose I bowed; but I was so astonished
at the drama, so overcome by the power and
genius of the whole, which far—*far* exceeded
anything I could have believed Helen capable
of producing, that I lost all consciousness of
where I was, and could only fast wipe away
my tears of sympathy and triumph.

I was recalled to other feelings by the energy
and exclamations of those upon whom, after
all, the fate of the play depended. The lady
who sat next to me, and who had been moved
to tears, said she was more than satisfied, and
requested her part might be sent to her immediately; then, folding herself in her cash-
mere, she murmured some words to me which
I did not hear, and bowing formally to the
manager, moved out of the room so silently,
that it was more like the gliding of a ghost
than the step of a living woman.

"If you had done as much for me, as you
have done for her," said the bright-eyed enamelled lady, advancing with a confident air, "I

should have thanked you most cordially ; but any part in such a play is an honour."

" *Any part!*" repeated a blue-eyed *blonde*, who was to be one of those confidential friends, not at all confined to the drama, but to be found hanging like parasites around the dwellings of the wealthy!—"Any part! why, madame, you have a lovely part!—I think it quite equal to the other. Any part!—I only wish you could be induced," she continued, addressing me, "to write me if it was half a length. I can do nothing with about six lines in five acts."

" I wish I could do as you request," I replied; "but I have no power; I came only to hear."

She shook her head, smiling sweetly in my face.

"Oh! you must not tell me that!—what can I do with six lines? and though madame complains, she has ten times as much, and two songs—those little *impromptu* songs that tell so much with the audience;—besides, I am 'discovered,' and you know what a disadvantage it is to be discovered. I never get a bit of applause when I am discovered; but if I come on, I am sure of a good round, and that gives me spirit."

"But your part does not want *spirit*, only *prudence*," said Madame.

"I hope I have enough of both," was the reply, as the blonde turned away with a deepened colour.

"Ladies, ladies," said the manager, whose talking to the prompter did not prevent his hearing and observing all that passed; "ladies ladies! you know it is not the length of a part which stamps its excellence. You can identify yourselves with characters of far less importance than these. The situations are admirable; and what is set down for you, as piquant and as expressive as if originated by yourselves. I consider the comedy of the play quite equal to the tragedy—superior indeed— for in the tragic parts the interest is rather created *for* the heroine than *by* her, whereas the dialogue and situation of the comedy works out its own purpose."

"I must say," observed a gentleman who appeared on very admirable terms with his

personal appearance, which he had eyed in
every possible position in a long pier-glass
opposite to where he sat, "I must say that
casting me, as I see you have done, in the low
comedy part, may prove very injurious to the
interests of the play, and indeed of the theatre.
I care nothing about myself; I never do; but
my friends !—the town !—the world ! my dear
sir, will be astonished ; and it may, as I said
before, injure the interests of the play and the
theatre. It *may* do so—that is all I fear."

"We must run the risk," replied the manager,
coolly.

"I'm sure, sir," said another, "Horace is a
mere walking gentleman without a word to
say—I never can get through that."

"Were you not engaged for the walking
gentlemen ?"

"And young lovers, sir," suggested the
actor, who certainly looked like anything but
a '*young*' lover.

"But the lover of this play is matured before
the play commences ; and I suppose you do
not wish to take that part from me," replied
the manager, with, I thought, very good

temper. The part he alluded to had evidently
been written for him, for there were allusions
in other parts of the drama, not only to his
personal appearance, but to his peculiarities—
"his knitted brows," which "even in joy were
drawn by care," and various other signs that
he was the hero of the plot. It seemed to me
that, though they all professed the greatest
admiration of the play, and repeated over and
over again their desire to serve its interests,
and the interests of the "management," caring
nothing, absolutely nothing, for themselves,
and laying every proposed change to their
desire to "do their duty;" still it was in fact
only of themselves they thought. I do believe
there was much self-deception in this—*much!*
for, to my astonishment, instead of being a
very artful, designing set of persons, they were
singularly the contrary; very deficient in tact,
for they could not hide their desire to shine;
and treated the applause of an audience as the
sole thing worth living for. They seemed
to consider the only shining lights in the world
to be the foot-lights, and the next best thing
to getting a new part, to be the ordering of a

new dress.   Instead of being the faded, *blaséd* sort of women I expected, they were remarkably fresh, and yet artificial.   I understood they came to a rehearsal three times a-week at least, and acted six nights out of the seven.   I called it very hard work, and wondered how I could have ever thought they gained their fame easily.   I do believe that each would have picked out the choice pieces from every part, and crammed them into their own—heaped them together, and then not have been quite satisfied unless the " good situations " accompanied the " spoken words."

" You promised me a part," said a very interesting girl of eighteen, with a fine expanded brow, and clear, direct-looking eyes; " you promised me a part, sir."

" I have given you one—first lady in waiting," replied the manager, still occupied with two strange men, the machinists I believe, for I heard about ' flats,' and 'flys,' ' changes,' and traps, banquets, and a fear lest some particular bandit should over-act his part.

" I have not one word to say, sir," persisted the girl, while a natural blush increased her beauty.

"Two very beautiful dresses, my dear, and you may order them of pink or blue, provided they are made true to the period."

"Dresses will not advance me in my profession, sir," she replied, adding—"you know I can speak—try me, sir; if I fail——"

"You fail!" added one of the gentlemen, throwing himself into a tragic attitude.

"If it were but one half-length, you promised me faithfully I should have a part, sir," she persisted, regardless of the interruption.

"And I have kept my word—you *have* a part."

Again she remonstrated, and the manager turned, I could not but think harshly, upon her.

"If ladies or gentlemen are dissatisfied with the cast of this play, let them throw up their parts. It is one of the most justly balanced dramas I ever read, and yet I have heard nothing but complaints."

Tears gathered in the young woman's eyes; she turned to the window to conceal them; no one heeded her, but the reproof seemed to have told; several turned away, others grouped together, and were loud in their praise of all they had just heard. I went to the young girl, she was sobbing bitterly, yet endeavouring to stifle her emotion. I said a few words of 'time' and 'difficulty,' and I hardly know what, but they had the effect of soothing her.

"If you would give me only three sentences," she said, "it would be enough to place me in a better position—a position I should not disgrace—do, do!—it would be a positive charity; only, if you write them for me, do not let them be transferred to another. You do not know how I have been kept back."

I assured her I could not write them, but I would speak to the author. She sank on the seat.

"Scenes are got up off as well as on the stage," whispered the enamelled lady, as she passed, glancing with the haggard expression of envy at the young girl, "but do not trust her to speak—she cannot." The bright cheerfulness of her face was gone while she uttered these words.

"Can it be," I thought, "that that woman,

who has been saturated with praise all her
days, now grudges to another to taste what
forms the staple commodity of her own life—
now, when the *furor* for fame ought to have
passed away. And I replied to myself, "Why,
this is the reason—twenty years before, she
could and would have afforded to be generous.
Now, in the evening of her days, and in
the decline of her attractions, she is terror-
stricken at every pretty face that comes
upon the stage, and will not play in the same
scene with youth or loveliness. *Yet* the world
says, that out of the profession her heart is
generous, and her judgments are kind; it is
only when the young and lovely come in contact
with herself, that she forgets everything but self.
Surely, surely it is not one woman in a thousand who grows old, gracefully, or honestly.

"What a profession it is," I thought, after
the once *naturally*-blooming woman passed from
the green-room, "what a profession it is to
create these feelings;" and then I felt how my
judgment stumbled at every step. Alas! the
profession *created* no such feelings. I could
not recal what I had observed in my pilgrimage

through life, and trace the existence of envy, hatred, or malice to the stage!

"Will it be impossible?" again urged the young actress, "quite impossible to give me even six lines—I am sure you could!"

"I have assured you," I replied, looking at her, fixedly, "that I had never even heard the drama until to-day; but I know the author, and if if it can be done she will do it."

"Then the author *is* a woman!—How wonderful!" said the gentlemen who had exclaimed "You fail!"

"I wish it had been you," observed the young girl mournfully, "for you look kind enough to give me a speaking part." The bit of flattery told even on me;—next to being thought beautiful in the pleasure of being considered kind; and I resolved to make it a point with Helen that she should have her wish.

I was about to retire, when the manager requested I would wait, and I did so.

To some of the performers I was introduced more particularly; and I perceived that the more stoutly I denied the authorship of the play, the more firm became their belief that I

was its author. I was exceeding perplexed
and annoyed at this, and told them with much
displeasure, that if they knew me better they
would find I was incapable of falsehood; but
one of them stoutly *maintained* there was no
falsehood in denying authorship; in short, he
made it appear that we had a right to tell un-
truths, if it were expedient to do so, about
anything written, and quoted Dr. Johnson as
an authority. This gentleman, I was told, was
the famous ' old man ' of the company : to me
he seemed a flaxen-headed, quick-witted,
cheerful, florid, young man, with a premature,
croaking, cranky, discontented voice. I could
not help asking if it were likely a woman at
my time of life, who had never written before,
could produce a drama; and seeing I was
really annoyed at having this new honour
thrust upon me, there were numerous bows,
and court'sies, and apologies, while all the time
I saw they did not believe one word I had
uttered.

The morning of the first rehearsal was
named; the manager, then, with much courtesy,
pointed out some very slight alterations, which

he requested the author to make. One speech,
in particular, he suggested it would be more
to the advantage of the play were it spoken by
—HIMSELF. I thought it particularly adapted
to the heroine; but he did not agree with me,
and, of course, as he was too great a man to
care about a speech, I was forced to think him
right. He said one thing which *did* perplex
me: he asked, "If the author would take care
of the Press?" and I answered, that "I
thought it was the duty of the Press to take
care of the author." "I see," he replied,
"that you really know nothing about these
matters."

I left the 'green-room' disabused of some
predjudices, yet perhaps having rather ex-
changed than overcome them, and with an inclination to see more of a class of persons who
were altogether different from all I had either
known or imagined; but this fancy was soon
overwhelmed by my desire to impart her
triumph to Helen. If I could have rushed to
her the moment the reading of the play was
concluded, my feelings might have been too
strongly expressed, and excited her hopes too

much.   As it was, I trembled when I thought of some of those to whom its destiny was consigned; and yet I became re-assured when I remembered that *their own fame* was wound up with that of the author; and if they failed to perform their parts rightly, *they* would lose their reputations.   The success or failure must affect those who undertook to embody the offspring of the poet's brain, yet, with one or two exceptions, what a *fearful* trust!

I saw Helen's face pressed against the glass as I drove to the door; she did not wait for the steps of the carriage to be let down, but sprang in at a bound, like a greyhound, and looked at me, without speaking a single word, clenching my hands so strongly within her own, that she gave me positive pain, her chest heaving and her eyes swimming in unshed tears.

"A complete triumph," I said.

"Yes, I see it," she whispered at last, "I saw it in your face, a complete triumph, as yet —as yet! then changing the subject, as if to get rid of her emotion, she continued rapidly—"My father has been restless and ill

ever since yesterday, but now he is asleep
again."

How she could write, or do anything but
feel, with that intense living sorrow before her,
is still to me a mystery; but why should I
refer to that single instance, when she herself
was the great mystery of my life? She was
exceedingly amused at the players fixing the
authorship on me, and absolutely wished me
to humour the deception, laughing at my
declaration that it would be an untruth;
like them, arguing that authors might tell
falsehoods about their authorship, and yet
not be guilty of falsehoods; and then enjoying
so much my not being able to understand
such reasoning. With prompt kindness she
wrote a few sentences for the hitherto name-
less first lady, and distinguished her by a
name, and then told me I must not come and
see her again until after the first rehearsal.
There was always something imperative about
Helen, which I used to fancy was simply the
power of a strong mind over a weak one—but
it had become habitual to her to command,
though it was the least offensive command a

human being could receive, and to energetic persons like myself, it is a relief to know what to do without the trouble of thinking much about it; still, I would in no wise give in to her humour about the authorship.

A day or two afterwards, I met Mr. Marley at Mr. Middleton's; my intercourse there had grown so constrained, that my single-minded young friend was perpetually asking me what was the matter, and I knew not what to say. I occupied myself with my netting before dinner, counting rows with Mrs. Dellamere, but soon giving up that, as I saw the good old lady did not like my doing three to her one. Mr. Marley took me down to dinner; on the way, bending his head, and smiling, as though he were saying the most pleasing thing in the world; he murmured—"If your fair friend does not propitiate, her play will not go a second night—the great comedy queen will never submit to Miss Delamotte's speaking while she is on the stage."

How could this man have obtained his information, and when it was obtained, what was it to him? I was more abstracted and

strange than ever, and Florence told me, jest-
ingly, in the drawing-room, that I was ceasing
to be even a 'NOBODY.'

The morning of rehearsal came. If a person
desire to be disgusted with his own play—no
easy matter—let him go to a rehearsal; it is
something quite awful to hear the parts read
over by the people, in the most unimpassioned
and even painfully careless manner; to see
them, (in an atmosphere thickened with dust,
and rendered still more impure by the linger-
ing fumes of oil, or the still more pernicious
gas,) only phantoms of the past night, hus-
banding their strength for the night that is to
come : and then the tottering scenery, lying
back against the walls, or hanging out of its
slips in an exhausted state, having no strength
of its own, ashamed of the thickened colours,
which at night it showed so proudly.   What a
mass of useless lumber it looks ! ropes dangling
from a ceiling, where a stray skylight permits
the thickly-moted sun-beams to wander on
the mimic stage ; a floor, looking as if only
swept by the dresses of the performers, and
seamed with ' traps,' opening to a deeper Pan-

demonium beneath 'the boards,' with draughts
enough to turn half a score of windmills, and
to which, at night, those who minister so suc-
cessfully to our pleasures are exposed when
every pore is opened by exertions which only
actors know.

It was astonishing to me how well they remembered their parts, considering the short
time they had studied them; and still more so,
how they could read them with so little sympathy; and I was provoked to find that all
the coming on and going off, which I fancied
must be dictated by the *feeling* of the persons,
was taught and called 'stage business'—yet
how natural it always seemed when seen from
the corner of my favourite box; while the
prompter annoyed me much, ever and anon
putting in his word—'giving the cue' I remember they called it—when I could not
think it was at all necessary; but what struck
me as the most singular thing of all, was
those full-grown people being so like children
—so particular about little things—so easily
amused by trifles—so delighted or annoyed by
their new dresses.

The manager took me to what he called 'a wing,' and said, that in consequence of some silly difference between Madame and Miss Delamotte, he feared that touching 'little bit,' so charmingly written, and so kindly intended, for the latter, must really come out, as Madame would not else appear with her on the stage. Marley's words echoed in my ears, but I stood firm to my purpose.

"If Madame objected," I repeated, again and again, "Miss Delamotte could take her part, she would *look it* much better."

If it be possible for a well-bred gentlemen to stare, the manager did stare at me. "I have just got the performers into such nice temper," he said; "and now this will put us wrong, as I have mentioned already, for when Madame is out of sorts she disconcerts us all."

"But leave her out," I persisted.

"You cannot understand the public," he said; "no play will go without her. She is now living on what she has been, which is frequently better than what she is. After a certain period, we all live upon our *reputations*; she is too wise to endanger hers by face to face contact with a pretty girl who promises talent ; really you must consider her feelings."

"Her folly, you mean."

" As you please ; only let the stage-manager strike out Miss Delamotte's part."

"Never ! " I said, firmly.

The manager looked aghast.

" Then permit the situation to be changed. Let her speak to some one else, so that she need not come to the foot-lights at the same time as Madame."

"I will consult the author," I replied.

" I assure you," he said—" I assure you, *as a friend*, that even the triumphant genius of the play would not carry it through without Madame."

I fear I looked incredulous.

" I see," said the manager, " that you and your unknown, the unknown and admired of the world, either do not understand, or do not care about, the minor methods that establish popularity.   H. L. has taken immense hold on the public ; but he or she has foes ; and if Madame is in the least disturbed, they will increase. I cannot be disinterested in the matter; but I feel doubly anxious for the success of a work of such high genius, cast so mysteriously upon the stream by one who, I must say, does not court success as far as I can see, but simply leaves it to stand or fall by its own merit!"

"And what else could she do?" I inquired.

There was the slighest possible play of the manager's eloquent mouth; and I felt that he thought my reply childish. He took my hand in a parental manner, and with a patronizing air said, "Certainly you and your *incognita* are unlike any other dramatists I have ever met, and my experience has been pretty large; however, I shall do everything in my power to secure a triumph. I think when you see the newspapers to-morrow, you will give me credit for good generalship—nothing like creating an excitement by a mystery.

CHAPTER III.

"From your good nature nought our authoress fears ;
Sure you'll indulge, if not the Muse, her years."

PRIOR.

———

AFTER seeing Helen, I drove home, and on my way, stopped at the newspaper and book shop of our hamlet—"send me, I said, all the morning and evening papers, to-morrow—all!"

"All," repeated the bewildered newsman.

"All."

"And to keep, madam?"

"Certainly, and I shall also want all the weekly papers."

"Thank you, madam, I wish every lady

took the same interest in the state of things, politics *would* look up then;" and after throwing as much respect into his bow, as if I had ordered a library; the news-agent plunged back into his den.

It would be impossible for me to describe what a restless night I passed, and how vainly I endeavoured to arrange or combine my thoughts, or oblige my reason to command my imagination. That some mysterious connection existed between Marley and Helen, I could not doubt; I was hag-ridden by the terror this knowledge inspired, and my aversion to him increased almost, I fear, to detestation, when I recalled the influence he seemed to possess, over those cousins whom I loved best of all the world.

I reasoned myself into a full belief in the moral and womanly superiority of that dear Florence; and yet my heart did not throb, or my eyes overflow for her, as they did for Helen. I cannot describe the earnestness of my devotion to Helen Lyndsey; her name was like a stroke of electricity, throbbing and exciting, savouring more of pain than pleasure.   I endeavoured to account for this superhuman interest, by recalling how long I had known her, how I pitied and sympathized with her, how I admired not only the justice but the generosity of her nature, for those qualities rather belonged to her *nature*, than to her *character*. I recalled the cordial and inspiring warmth of her affections, her devotion to her father, her industry. I would have it that I considered her genius as *second* to these better things. I tried to convince myself—while hunting over the newspaper columns for the paragraphs, which the manager told me were to herald her play that I despised fame, and hated notoriety.   I went on schooling myself in self-deception ; I kept Helen's faults, and one fault more than all the rest, out of sight, hoping to forget their existence.   In short, though I struggled against the growth of what was positive idolatry to this marvellous girl—I struggled feebly—I found I continued adding, and adding to the triumphs I anticipated for her —even while my lips framed lectures against vain glory. Oh, how I preached against

' vanity of vanities ; ' how repeated to myself,
again and again, that sentence. Yet I read and
re-read those paragraphs of the manager with
such pleasure! The insinuation, the delicious
mystery, the hint—far off the mark—the
assumed knowledge, the ' confidential communication,'—all tending to excite that
species of public curiosity which gapes after
novelty or singularity, that runs after ' lions '
—roar they ever so ' mildly.'—not because of
their real ' attributes,' but because of their
being talked of, far more than their talking, or being talked tò.

I speculated upon ' consistency,' and
questioned myself whether it were a reality,
or a romance. I was conscious of such
extraordinary and contemptible inconsistency
in myself, enjoying as I did the repute of
being ' a still dear NOBODY, who was always
the same '—that I could not reconcile myself to
myself—or myself to anyone else. Had I
been a man, the world would have said I was
in love with Helen—as it was, I was vividly
alive to her faults, and yet, such were her
qualities—such was her fascination, such her

genius, that the more I thought of her, and
blamed myself for thinking, the more entirely
did she absorb every faculty, not only of my
mind, but of my affections. I almost shame
to confess that all belonging to Florence,
even Florence herself, faded, as delicate
colours pale before the burning rays of the
glowing sun. I told myself that her
destiny was sealed—that she would marry
Mr. Marley—that I could do nothing to
prevent it. I tried to believe that she
could do without me—that she did not want
me. I even dared once to think her capricious
—she! the fondest, most faithful of God's
bright creatures. My mind also really became
distracted by the turn matters took in the
theatre; the lady whom I have called 'Madame,' depending on her long-achieved and
long-sustained ascendancy over the public,
determined to throw up her part, unless the
few lines given to the young actress's earnest
entreaty, were cut out; when I represented
this to Helen, she clenched her little hand on
her grey goose quill, grasping it like a dagger
—"look," she exclaimed, "I will submit to

no tyranny. I am young and struggling myself; and though I have never seen her,
I will not suffer that poor girl's beauty and
talent to continue wrapt in grave-clothes,
merely to minister to the pampered whim of
an insolent woman."

"Strengthen this good resolve, my friend,
strengthen it, for it is right. It is right!" I
said; "and yet urged by the prudence which
whispers that *this* is your first great step in
life —— "

"No, no," she said; "it is not my first
step, call it my first *stride*, if you will;
but my first step was made long ago—on the
half-broken slate, at Hampstead—when the
shrewish persecutions of my cruel mother
drove me often to shelter beneath the goose-
berry bushes—the old crowded, cankered
things, whose thorns entered into my flesh—
less sharp were they, than her words! No—
I will *not* change."

"The manager says —— " I interrupted.

"I do not care a straw what he says! He
says, of course, everything he can to keep his
people in good humour; let him send back the

play if he likes—there, don't teaze me about it. I have got the sweetest wreath of jessamine to wear on my first night."

"You are not going to encounter," I exclaimed, earnestly, "the actual house that night? you cannot mean to try your nerves by such a fearful ordeal; you will betray yourself."

"Betray myself," she repeated, and she turned the full radiance of her face upon me, which clouded as she spoke, "Betray myself, no, there is no fear of that! Alas! alas! I should have lived to little purpose, during the last desperate years if now I could betray myself. Would deadly-night-shade," she added, while taking the wreath of jessamine out of its box—"would deadly-night-shade be a more appropriate head dress than this?"

"What a strange creature you are, Helen!"

"Ay! all are considered strange who differ from each other."

"But, about this discontented woman, Helen."

"Which?" she said, with an arch smile; "did you ever know one of us contented?"

"Madame, I mean."

"What does it signify? If the play is worth playing, the manager will have it; if it is played, Madame will be *perdu* on the horns of dilemma; the pretty face on one side, removed from before the public on the other! But, believe me, she will not lose the opportunity of wearing three new dresses, and singing two songs—her *amour propre* will be her tempter."

"But Helen——"

"Well! this is contradictory! you first turned my feelings towards this poor girl, and now you are terror-stricken at the consequences. How many things are lost to those who will not strike the *second* blow?"

It never was any use to reason with her, and now I knew she was right—and yet the wrong, seemed the better reason. I was cowardly enough to regret the interest I had taken in the young actress!

Helen regretted nothing—"the public spoils its favourites," she exclaimed, "but I will not pander to its mismanagement—the part is still open to madame, if madame desire it

—if not, let the manager get another first lady, and give madame's part to this Miss Delamotte—I tell you I have *faith* in my play, no high purpose was ever achieved without that faith—there are numbers who *will* hear H. L.'s play—let there be a riot!—only fancy my creating a riot in the great metropolitan theatre."

" But Helen ! "

"Enough about it, " she repeated, stamping her little foot, "if Miss Delamotte plays first lady, she shall speak her speech in the right place—and speak it all—if she does not play *that*—she shall play *Josephine*— and let *madame* look to it——"

That very evening the manager found out my cottage at Hampstead; he told me that madame was in a fury; that she had said so much, he did not know how she could retract, and accept the part; that whether she filled it or not, he would not risk its reputation by entrusting it to my *protegée*—whose talent had never been tried—but that there would certainly be a riot in the house, if she did not play; that one or two of the news-

papers had hinted as much; that madame had
great influence with the press; that he did not
like to treat her ill———————"

Oh, how weary I was!— " ' treat her ill,' "
I said—" she can command her original part,
the dresses and songs, and everything she
desires !—"

The manager smiled, and shook his head,
"but her *empire*, her empire of beauty is in-
terfered with; surely, madam, you can understand how hard it is for a woman to endure
being side by side with the freshness of youth,
when her own is fading; to see admiring opera
glasses levelled at a new face, passing over
hers as if it had never been ! to find the ' first
appearance ' set forth in half a column—while
she has hardly a paragraph.   Oh, dear lady!
—surely you can understand how hard it is
for a beauty to resign her commission into the
hands of a junior officer—"

I replied, that never having been a beauty,
I was an ill judge of such matters—but that
the author was firm to her purpose—and he
must do his best.

This woman's war occupied more thought and

time, and talk than the play itself; but the
manager was in an ecstasy at one time of hope,
at another of despair, at its having become
town-talk—the box office was beset by people,
in and out of carriages bespeaking 'places'
for the first night of 'H. L.'s play;' the
partisans of 'madame' looked 'thundering,'
and applauded to the very echo, whenever
she appeared upon the stage; the papers
poured forth little mysterious paragraphs
of 'on dits,' and 'hints,' and 'expecta-
tions.' Florence caught the excitement, and
secured a box—Marley took care it should
be as far from the stage as possible. Helen
worked away •at other literary matters, as
if nothing were going to take place out of
the ordinary course of things; but she grew
pale and thin, her movements were more rapid,
and feverish—she insisted on my being present
at the rehearsals, to which 'madame' did not
come; she would neither resign her part, nor
attend to it.

Once standing at the wing and looking
through the murkiness of the house, con-
trasting in my own mind the difference be-

tween the daylight and midnight aspect of the
mimic world, noting the sunbeams that strayed
in from some far · away skylight, creating
such curious effects, now calling forth the
rainbow tints of a chandelier, then drawing
out the crimson of a curtain, forming an arrow
of light, passed and repassed by floating
moats, mere dusty atoms, which in that
magic beam sparkled like jewels, listening to
one thing, and looking at another, one moment
sadly out of tune, with the small jealousies
of those to whom the stage was all the world
—sick at heart—for the wearied, soiled, and
worn out ballet-girl, who at night shone in
gossamer and spangles—disgusted with the
worse than nothings, which old fops poured
into the ears of young fools—tired by repetitions—provoked by delays! Once I stood, as
I have said at the wing, wondering how it was
the scenery did not fall, or the traps open,
while all the time the rehearsal proceeded :
Miss Delamotte, catching her cue, and deliver-
ing her single speech, with the earnestness and
zeal of one whose all is cast upon a die;
when, looking to see why a particular sunbeam

did not fall upon as particular a silken tassel, which, somehow, escaped from its brown holland, had been shining like a huge ruby in the light, my eyes caught a face retreating back into the royal box. It was Helen's. The sunbeam again toyed with the tassel; again was its line broken—by Marley! Were the weird sisters performing their acursed incantations in the broad daylight, reviving my senses by their treacherous shows?

"You are ill," said Miss Delamotte, " this atmosphere, this fatigue is too mnch for you, or did my speech affect you. Oh, I should be so certain of success if it did!"

I could not flatter, but replied, " did you see anyone in the Royal box?"

"Certainly, two persons, a lady and a gentleman; do you know them ? "

" I fear I know neither," I replied bitterly, " have you lived long enough in the world to feel that you know—"

" What? "—enquired the girl.

" Nothing"—

When I was going out a few minutes after I met Miss Delamotte at the door, large tears trembled on her eye lashes. "I hoped you would have been pleased with me," she said. "I had taken such pains with the speech, but I see you are disappointed."

"Nay," I replied, "not at all disappointed —I never heard it!"

CHAPTER IV.

" Come: I will crown thee with a poet's bough;
Mine is an humble branch, yet not in vain
Given, if the few I sing shall not disdain
To wear the little wreaths that I bestow."

PROCTER.

I TOLD Helen I had seen her in the King's
box, and wondered how she got there, and she
answered rapidly, that Mr. Marley procured
her the *entrée*.

Any one almost, she believed, could get there
at rehearsal, if known to the manager, and he
knew everybody—

" Was her secret safe with him ?"

" Of course; there were others who could
keep secrets as well as NOBODY"—smiling such

E 2

a smile—" Oh yes, her secret was safe with him."

"But, my dear Helen!"

"Well!"

"This Marley—"

" Ay—is he not handsome?"

"You know he is going to be married to Florence."

"Poor Florence!"

"Why do you say 'poor Florence?'"

"Because you say she is going to be married to Marley."

"Does he deny it?"

"Oh, no why should he deny it. It is an admirable match, a grand *coup* for him—but do not let us give words, or time, or thoughts to anything but the great event, which elevates me now. I wish the night was come."

"Do you not also wish it gone."

"Gone! no, why should I wish it gone?" Every fibre of her exquisitely moulded frame dilated in anticipated triumph, while with flashing eyes and burning cheeks, she added— "I know that play must succeed with or without madame—it *must*, I cannot be ig-

norant of the power I have in the closet to put
thoughts and words into action. I will not
have you *look* a doubt, " she continued passionately, " if it did not triumph it would kill
me. Since the time when I named my high-
back chairs, Ferdinand and Miranda, when
the mighty words of our great Dramatist
were stamped upon my brain ; and I left my
bed during the brief nights of moonlight, to
act 'The Tempest,' speaking all the speeches
myself, and moving my chairs into dramatic
situations, in my veriest childhood, I framed
this great resolve, to write a play, to see it
acted, and feast upon the plaudits of the
world."

I thought how much greater was the
triumph she had already achieved, by the
patient self-denial, which, amid privations —in
a land of strangers—taught her to pay her
father's debts; but she was then out of tune with
all the patient virtues—dazzled by the consciousness of her own genius, and fevered by an
appetite for fame. She drew also a good omen,
from the fact, that her father had been for
some nights more tranquil, and during the day,

less restless and impatient; the hope mingled
with her dream of glory, was one of her father's
recovery.   She steadily refused to see any of
the puffs preliminary, which heralded her play,
though she derived infinite pleasure, from hearing
that every seat in the house was disposed of,
and enjoyed with mischievous delight, the news
that madame kept the manager in a fearful
state of uncertainty   " To act or not to act,"
that was the question.   She positively revelled
in the dilemma, and seemed disappointed when
on the morning of the first night—madame suc-
cumbed, on condition that Miss Delamotte was
to remain *veiled*, while she was on the stage. I
did not, however, venture at first to detail to
Helen this act of petty tyranny; she would
have risen against it, and had become almost
fretful at the idea of the contest being given
up.   I found she had been to the theatre and
secured a private box for herself; how little
did the box-keeper imagine who was to be its
tenant. She determined to go alone—nor
would she even tell me at which side of the
house this mysterious box was situated.

I could not have shared mine with any living

creature. Drury Lane was crowded with carriages. I got quietly into the theatre, and as I stole along, I felt I was pointed at, and those at the stage door who could presume an acquaintanceship, wished me success. The roll of carriages, the hoarse screams of the 'links,' seemed to my over-wrought nerves like human thunder. I could not speak, or exchange one civil word, for the many congratulations, which met me on the stairs, and which I tried to assert I had no right to receive. I looked upon the pit—one huge hive of human beings. I did not know how much a pit full of men was prized, and longed to see some gentle women's faces among those terrible men, who seemed to be all critics. The gallery too, was crammed —and silent, the boxes filling rapidly—occassionally a box-door slammed, or the last seat slipped from the keeper's hand and fell with a crash, or there was a rustle in the pit—some weak or fastidious man complaining of the pressure; but all seemed waiting to see the clearing up of a mystery. Moats floated before my eyes, resolving themselves into forms, long past. Helen! with her slate—

Helen! clinging to her father—Helen! her dripping hair folded around her throbbing brow, toiling with brain and hand to pay her father's debts—Helen! triumphing in a power —*the* power to quicken the beatings of every heart within that arena—to draw tears from every eye—to nerve each hand for applause— to rouse each voice, as the voice of one, in a long shout of approbation—the little child that had crouched within my arms to do all this!

I pressed my face into my hands and prayed—I bent my knees in supplication behind the crimson folds which shut out that world. I tried to put it from me; although but one prayer—that whatever was best for HER might come to pass; sob after sob arose from my heart—my hands were soaked in tears. There was a loud clapping, then a hush.

The manager spoke the prologue—the rich music of his voice propitiated favour; the beauty of his elocution was in itself so harmonious, that every ear drank it in with delight— at one moment it was confidence, at another entreaty—he was gone. There was music then, but it was out of tune while the tones of that delicious voice floated on the air.

The play began—at first I dared not look upon the stage ·I could hardly hear—my senses were benumbed. The pit caught a point in the second scene, and applauded to the echo—another sound, set going by hands, heated with enthusiasm—then I breathed— I could see and hear.

Burst after burst succeeded—the pit tired of its happy labour.

Madame never looked more lovely, though I heartily wished her away—she was the canker in the rose—the mildew on the peach. I could not separate her public talent from her private character.

Miss Delamotte came forward to the footlights; the veil floated over her lovely face as some envious cloud conceals the beauty of a landscape. She spoke, and the tremulous voice —gaining confidence from its own sweetness— became more audible—more touching with each word. One of her many gifts was a voice of exquisite expression; it flowed from between her lips without an effort, clear, ringing, and distinct, and yet with a light and feathery tone. Helen had enriched that speech, short as it was, with jewelled thoughts—every sentence was a gem ; and the crowded house kept in its mighty breath, catching the pearls which came forth in rich profusion.

Suddenly taking advantage of a pause, which was to bring out 'a point'—the very crown of the ' situation,' and while the young actress, true to her compact, folded the veil still more closely over her face, a clear, distinct voice exclaimed, " *Unveil !*" I trembled from head to foot. I grasped the curtain with both hands. The voice was Helen's! Instead of this producing a tumult, the men in the pit seized the idea, and repeated it in various tones of entreaty and command There stood madame : I fancied she flushed, even through the enamel, and her beautiful face became convulsed. She turned from the audience with a gesture of hatred and contempt; but the next moment returned beaming with smiles ; while poor Miss Delamotte seemed ready to sink into the stage.

" Unveil—unveil !" echoed from all parts of the house, amid thundering hands, and noisy calls for ' silence.'

I was in an agony. I felt that Helen had perilled her own play. The excitement increased to a tumult, until its origin was forgotten; when some men in the stage-box returned to it, and the cry 'Unveil' was renewed with redoubled vigour.

While the young actress trembled in the storm, madame advanced, and, lifting the veil from the poor girl's head, where it had rested on a crown of roses, placed it on her own, shadowing her face with the transparent gauze with one hand, while with the other she led Miss Delamotte to the foot-lights. Never was there a greater evidence of tact, never, on or off the stage, a finer 'bit' of acting; it was perfect! As if to give Miss Delamotte time to recover *her* self-possession, she sang as if she could not choose but sing—the *refrain* of an old ballad, which had preceded Miss Delamotte's speech· This drew down 'a round of well-earned applause, until the house rang again. And then still shrouded by the veil of her adoption, she awaited the reception of the words, in an attitude so statuesque, and yet so perfectly natural, that it was worthy of being

studied by Canova. The young actress gave
the words better than before; and they were
fully appreciated. This scene terminated by
a ball, and during the dancing (which was only
the cotillion movement, then giving way in
fashionable circles to the quadrille), I could
hear the rapid questioning, as to *who* the
young actress was, where she had been, where
she came from; while scores of *lorgnettes*
followed her movements. This seemed to ir-
ritate madame's party, who got up a call to
her to 'unveil,' a call repeated by the gallery,
ever ready for a riot, and hushed by others;
what followed, threatened to turn the scene
into ridicule. Miss Delamotte, resolved not
to be out-done in generosity, caught the
floating gossamer as she passed madame in
the dance, and replaced it in its original position. And madame suffered the woman so far
to triumph over the actress, as to *show* her
satisfaction by coming forward to the foot-
lights, and curtseying, *not* with her usual
grace and dignity, for she was nervous and excited, and looked radiant with triumph; but
her curtsey was more eloquent than words.

The two ladies hand in hand, as lovingly as twin sisters, were enfolded by the veil. If 'all the world's a stage' I thought to myself; if "all the world's a stage, and all the men and women merely players," what have *I* been living for and who amongst? Can this be an epitome of life, and all the loving cordiality, and pretty gracious ways passing between women, are they but veiled 'motives'—but startling 'effects,' is there no substance in them? Even amid that tumult, that thunder of applause which brought down the curtain at the end of the second act, I would have been their monarch; I could not avoid the feeling—humbling though it was!

The manager entered the box unperceived.

"Why did you cry out unveil?" he said, "why did you peril the play, from regard to that girl?"

His indignant eyes met mine with all the fierce magic of their strength and beauty, like the eyes of a sorcerer—me!—who hardly dared to call my breath my own in that atmosphere—who had shrank behind the curtain lest I should by chance be seen, although no one would look at me while my heart was beating in

my throat, and literally taking away the little
power I had of utterance—it seemed so suddenly
appalled by the charge, as to cease beating altogether.

"We know," he continued, having soothed
himself down, " that women of genius
are sometimes a little eccentric, and prettily
wilful, but pray do not risk an interruption
of that sort again ; but for madame's exquisite tact we might have lost the house—it was
wonderfully done—she is an astonishing creature ! three artists have followed her to the
green-room to entreat her to let them paint
her as a veiled Venus ; and Miss Delamotte
has escaped to her dressing-room ; though it is
under the stage, the ladder is besieged by admirers. You see, position is everything ; the
own has gazed at Miss Delamotte in silent
parts and groups during the last two years,
but never *saw* her until to-night." The manager had a habit of looking down while he
spoke, and, then suddenly flashing his eyes
upon the persons he addressed, as if to take
them by surprize. It was painful to feel so
watched, yet, confused as I was, I perceived

that numbers in the pit, seeing him talking to
me, were reconnoitering, and that there was a
general move of 'eye-sight' towards the box I
occupied. "I must again congratulate you," he
said, "and vanish, for I am to be ' discovered.' "
In the next act he turned back, after fastening
the box-door, to entreat me to forgive him, if
in his admiration of the play, and zeal for my
success, he had said more than was becoming
of the risk I had run, and, with an air of
gallant respect, kissed my hand, or rather my
glove, and, then as he would call it, ' vanished '
without my being able to utter a syllable,
panting as I was to deny his inference, and
trembling with indignation at being disbe-
lieved. I rushed to the box-door to recal
him; my cloak and shawls, which I had
thrown upon the chairs, sprang up before me, and Helen, shaking them off as
the columbine of the night shakes off her
first garments in a pantomime, stood
there — as the heroine of a novel always
does when least expected—bright, beautiful,
triumphant, and yet full of merry malice at
my discomfiture. She laughed outright at my

displeasure and perplexity, and was as pleased
as a child would have been, at having got into
the box without my knowledge—she was in
ecstacy at the idea of my being called for as the
author of the play, to curtsey from the box. In
another instant she enveloped herself in my
draperies, and fixed her eyes—(I have a passion for beautiful eyes to this day, no matter
the colour, so they are large, deep-set, and
dewy; the physiognomist may take all the
rest of the face, the phrenologist all the head,
so they give me but the eyes! and such eyes
as Helen's!)—she fixed those eyes upon the
scene, and remained for a time immoveable.

All is long past and gone, that play but
seldom acted, not so much because there are
no ' great stars' to do it justice, in parts, but
because it was so evenly written, giving to
each actor enough, and requiring that to be
well done; so that there is uo efficient company now a-days to render it attractive; but
every scene, every line, every look, every
movement, was so impressed upon me, that I
can recall them now, and even fancy that I
hear the anxious gasp, the trembling sigh, the

very beating of that high heart, as the creator of the scene—a young fragile woman—followed all with ears and eyes, and heart. When peal after peal of approbation resounded through the house—she rose gradually from her crouching position, her child-like figure expanding with triumph; then, when all was hushed, she sank again, until only those bright eyes sparkled in the darkness; the curtain at the last came down amid a whirlwind of applause. She crept to my side, and buried her face in my lap. I could hear her sob, and feel she had given way. "My own NOBODY," she whispered: "only you must know this."

The manager spoke the epilogue—the pit thinned off—the front row altogether disappeared (in those days, it was filled by the critics).

Some one knocked at my box-door. "One moment!" exclaimed Helen; every trace of agitation vanished from her face. She sat by my side in the shadow—a quiet little girl, with a meek, shy expression of countenance—her head bent, as if by the masses of hair, which fell in rich folds and waved over her shoulders.

Again it was the manager—all bows and
triumph, and congratulation; he seemed to
wish to get me to the front of the box. Every
head was turned towards us—the applause
renewed—for the people recognized the hero
of the drama, and their long-established favourite.

"Young lady," he said imploringly, addressing Helen, "cannot *you* prevail on the
star—the 'H. L.' of our literature—the poet
—the philosopher—the dramatist—the successful dramatist, to stand forth, just for a
moment, and with one smile, gratify such an
audience. Your friend's silence this evening,
has confessed the suspected truth—it will be a
grand *coup* to solve the mystery—*here*—in the
great field of her success, proving the wonderful strength which could support a first representation. I pray you prevail on the author
to stand just one moment in front of the box."

Helen made no reply, but rose and with the
composure of one who had traced the foot-lights
for half a century, did as he wished the author
to do; he did not, however, notice the movement; but continued to entreat me to do,
what she had done.

She broke into a low elfin laugh—the mocking laugh of her childhood—and in childlike delight, whispered—"You may tell." Then fixing her eyes upon the manager, prepared to exult in his astonishment. As I dreaded what he desired—'a scene'—I drew forward the curtain, so as to shut out the audience; and, taking Helen's little hand within my own, presented her to him in due form.

I saw he did not believe one word I said ; the only idea he seemed to have, was a species of indignation that I could imagine it possible he could be so easily deceived. Helen, feverish and excited, endeavoured to seem calm and careless, answered one or two questions with much self-possession—had no desire to be presented to the ladies in the green-room, though she enjoyed the idea of a crowd at the box-door, to congratulate 'NOBODY.' At the moment Mr. Marley entered, and not even his perfect breeding could conceal his agitation. He wished Helen joy of her success in a tone which conveyed rather regret than satisfaction; added his testimony to mine that she was really the 'H. L.' doomed to wear the laurel ; whispered to me, that Florence wished to see me, and that he would escort Miss Lyndsey home, which I refused to permit, sending a loving message to Florence, and adding that I would call on her in the morning.

"It is disagreeable enough, my own friend," she whispered; "but I could not talk to you to-night: so go to Florence; give her my love. *Now* I will know her—*now*, when I cannot disgrace her, or be *suspected of wanting help from a rich relation.* Marley will see me home. How shocked you look! We are old friends: I am quite safe with Marley. He hates me," she added, in an under tone, "and —I—hate him!"

She took his arm!

"Florence cannot want to see me to-night," I whispered; "and I will not suffer you to leave the theatre, alone, with any man."

I followed her, the bewildered manager constituting himself my escort. I do not know how we got through the crowd, or crossed the stage, half suffocated with the smell of oil and gunpowder; for the after-piece had commenced, and they were storming Seringapatam, and the dark-painted troops were making furious efforts,. with cimeters and small arms, on mimic towers, and gongs were beating, and sultanas screaming on the stage, and flirting at the wings ; and that lovely Miss Delamotte, in a turban, and with darkened brows, was in the act of falling in with a group close to the prompter's box.

"Thanks to you," said the manager, *sotto voce*, to me, "this is the last time she will have to go on in the after-piece, except in character. That veiling and unveiling has made her fortune."

The stage door was crowded.

"Will I find yer honour's carriage? I'll have it up before any of them—will I—will I yer honour?" said an Irish voice, with a poverty-stricken link, that gave a mere ray of light, while sturdier fellows flashed their large flambeaux, adding smoke to the London fog, which half concealed the carriage and horses, as if by some continued dramatic illusion. Helen started at the voice, and turned round to look at the speaker. He let his link drop, and with a shriek, fell upon his knees at her side.

" Oh, then, it's yourself, darling !—praise be to heaven—it's you that are in it—you! ' *Avourneen Ma chree !* '—You ! grown from a *colleen das*, into a fine young lady ! Oh, then, let your voice ring music on my heart; say you remember Jerry !"

" My kind, good friend," said Helen, in her old earnest voice—"I'm so glad to see you, particularly to-night—you both—both—who so dearly, truly loved me," she added, turning to me.

" An old follower of the family," suggested the manager ; " those people are full of dramatic talent—fine, noble, brilliant people, madam—the finest people in the world—*they are all actors !* "

Helen and Marley had disappeared in the crowd ; Jerry rose from his knees, with Helen's purse, which she had thrust into his hand.— " She called me her friend," repeated Jerry— " *her friend.*—I didn't want her money,"—his eyes met mine—"I did not," he repeated. " I come here sometimes, just for a bit of divarsion—Hampstead's so dull—in the season, and I knew Miss Florence was here to-night,

and I thought you too had forgotten me."
There was no time to let the reproach sink
into my heart, as it ought to have done; the
manager was entreated by one of the messen-
gers, to come immediately to his room, where
a royal duke was waiting. I was too glad to
get rid of him, and follow Helen; I, in my
turn, followed by Jerry. I jostled through the
crowd, anxious, fevered, miserable—it was
all chaos to me—I could not define or arrange
a single thought, or describe a sensation;
elated as I had been at one moment by her
triumph, I was torn the next by the most
painful apprehensions as to what could be her
connection with Marley.

"There they are!" exclaimed Jerry.

"Where?"

"There; she's just got into that carriage,
and he after her. Stop, coachman, for the
lady!—no, they're off!" The carriage passed
close to the *trottoir*; she saw me distinctly,
for she kissed her hand, and *he* bowed.

"That gentleman's very like—somebody,"
soliloquized Jerry, as composedly as if he were
on Hampstead Heath by moonlight; "and

yet he ain't—and still he is—it ain't the eyes,
no—maybe it's the nose; the nose is a fine
steady feature to take a likeness from, it's
always the same—always—till it turns to
snuff; the mouth—no, it's not the mouth; the
sit of the head on the shoulders; the smile—
oh, bad luck to it!—no; the figure—sure he's
a good head taller—it ain't the figure, anyhow.
See here, lady dear, and if you can't tell me
I'll ask the priest, are devils ever like angels?
Well, dear, anyhow, it's time I called your
carriage, for you can't stand much longer."

She was gone without *me*, and with *him*!

CHAPTER V.

" ———All that is great in thought,
That strikes at once, as with electric fire,
And lifts us, as it were, from earth to heaven,
Comes from the heart : and who confesses not
Its voice as sacred, nay, almost divine,
When inly it declares on what we do,
Blaming, approving ?"

ROGERS.

Oh what a long and dreary night that was!
—how different from the triumph I had anticipated—or rather, how different the result of
that triumph on myself. For Helen the success
was undoubted. That dearly-loved child,
whom I had shielded from a mother's
unkindness—whose indications of genius I

had discovered and fostered—whose faults I
had combated honestly, even while in my
own mind I excused them—whose image had
grown into my household god—whom I had
prayed for, earnestly, tenderly, unceasingly—as
if—I do believe what I say—as if she had been
laid on my bosom by Almighty Goodness, my
own child! That darling, that soul's idol, had
accomplished in youth-hood—the youth-hood
of a girl—what literary manhood had so often
failed to compass; and yet, while my heart
beat and glowed with delight (with, it might
have been, an unholy pride), I was stricken
down by the unaccountable and perilous influence that Marley exercised over her. How
was it?—what was it?—why was it?—he
—the betrothed of Florence Middleton. I
could not solve the mystery—I had no clue—
no ray of light; I thought of her high soul,
her noble impulses and rejoiced:—of her rash-
ness, and of continental habits and influences,
and trembled. A child, a very child, with
such a father, abroad; alone; I questioned
my own heart closely; could it be that such
phantoms were called up by fretful selfishness,

or wounded self-love, because (so it might be) I
was no longer her first, her only friend? Did
I want still to be her *only* friend? Had she
so filled my heart, that not only could I receive no other into its sanctuary, but wish her to
stand alone with me in the wide world? It was
just the grey dawn of morning, when I found
out *myself* in that great selfishness; humbled
and ashamed, I felt how often I had prayed for
Helen, how seldom for myself; what right
had I to doubt her?—how dared I to judge?
I remembered my own youth, its rash pre-
sumptions; I, so calm and quiet now; I
prayed meekly, on my knees; I prayed for
confidence in what I knew was unerring wisdom, I prayed, as men pray for life, to be
directed, to be guided, rather as a child
blindfold, than by the vague light of my own
reason—I began by praying for myself; I
ended praying for her; but, as I arose, I felt,
as it were, my better self return—calmed, concentrated, seeing nothing more, but trusting,
believing the time would come when I should see
and understand all; and, tired out, I threw
myself on my bed, and slept long and soundly,

the deep sleep induced by fatigue of body and of spirit.

The following day, Hampstead Heath might have been thought to be on fire; people—who, in those primitive times of early hours, never ventured a morning call before twelve, and kept such accurate count of visits paid and received, that 'caste' would be inevitably lost, were a visit made out of 'turn'—now rushed to each other's houses, to tell and hear, and hear and tell, before the breakfast-tables were despoiled of their morning 'freight' of good things. As usual, upon such occasions, the 'hearers' were in the minority—all talking, all telling. Jerry was my first visitor. I might well be ashamed to see him; for I ought to have communicated to him something of the chance he had of seeing Helen, only I so feared his warmth of heart, and want of discretion. I need not have done this—I fear I made the excuse to myself—and that the truth was, I had not thought of him. With rounded eyes and open mouth, and a countenance eager and flushed, he stammered forth the question—" Was it true as gosp'l,

that Miss Helen, his own Miss Helen, the
'darlint' he had loved all his life—the poor
masther's daughter—was it thrue that she
made all kinds of *poethry* out of her own head?
that she had made a play—the play that all
the world was at last night ; was it *thrue* that
she would have *lashins* of money; that all the
great people in London would fight who should
have her at their houses?   It seemed but a
drame ; and he could shut his eyes, and think
it so; only that they had it at Jack Straw's,
through the postman, that it was Miss Helen,
and no other ; and sorra a one would believe
it, until he said he saw her with his own two
eyes.   At last, when he was fairly exhausted,
I told Jerry it was all true, that there was no
doubt that Miss Helen was a STAR—that she
was a woman of genius.

Jerry interrupted me.

" What did you say she was, ma'am dear?'

" A woman of genius."

" Just one word, my lady; is a woman of
genius *all as one* as a man of genius ? "

" Yes, pretty nearly the same."

" They used to say in the place I come

from, that the eldest son of the master I was
born under, was a great ganius, and that was
the reason he never did a ha'porth of good for
himself or any one else.   And the mistress
called a mad horse she had *Ganious*, just out
of derision of poor master Harry, and to try to
break him of it, but it was no use.   And the
whole family of the Lawlors, of Castletown
Lawler, they were *ganiouses*, and you may look
a long midsummer day for them through the
ruins of the fine place they war born to, and
not find as much as a handful of meal where
you'd have thought guineas grew as plenty
as blackberries.   And the craythurs themselves, lonely and *could*, in strange church
yards, or their white bones rowling under the
waves, or may be the worst of all, forgetting
themselves with those who had neither blood
nor breeding, paying for their dinner with a
song, or a story, held up to make sport for
every fool that had a guinea.   Or Miss
Mary Burke! I heerd tell about her, and
saw her *once*, a wild *extravagated* gentlewoman, more tormenting in herself than poor
Mrs. Lyndsey, and every one skitting and laugh-

ing at her, they called her an out-an-out
ganious, though she had neither blood, bone,
nor beauty, and not a grain of sense in a bushel
of words; and all the public stared at her;
it's mighty well for a man to go into the public
line; but I never could abide it in a woman.
To be sure there's a deal in the differ, and
I'm a fool not to see it, and worse, not to
be out of my senses at the glory of the fame,
and the fame of the glory; but the thing I
want is that darlin, Miss Helen, in the
bower, where nothing but God's sunbeams
could look in upon her! not set upon a pole,
for all the world to be staring at. And no one
can tell me a word of the master—the good
master—sufferin' all his life for an early transgression."

"What transgression, Jerry?" I inquired.

Through the deep mahogany-colour, that
the sun had burned into his cheeks, Jerry
blushed, a deep crimson, but his national
tact did not forsake him. " Look, lady dear!
I'm not myself—it's not me that's in it—I'm
made up of lies and blunders, I don't know
what I'm saying—I'm so full of my own trans-

gressions. My shadow's not like me, and my
tongue isn't the one I was born with. I've
been so lame with the rheumatis, and so
bothered with the lightness in my head, that I
couldn't keep near them good Middletons (the
heavens be their bed!)—only came out for
peace and fresh air to the hayloft; and then I
was so uneasy in meeself, on account of a
drame I had, that I had no help for it, but to
go back, then and there, to the town; and
thought I'd see the company and Miss Florence,
and, as it was foggy, take a hand at the links,
to accommodate the gentry, and sarve a poor
boy, a friend I have, who wasn't able to handle
his own link last night, and his wife and children at home hungry; she came upon me like
a flash of lightning; and everything we heerd
since has been over me again and again, all as
one as the same combustible; and no sleep,
only on my two bare knees, praying hard and
fast for her and the masther. And now,
ma'am dear"—added Jerry, who might well be
out of breath, between his energy and his
eloquence—" and now, ma'am dear; " and he
looked mysteriously round the room, shut the

door, and withdrew the curtains, so as to peep
out of the window—" do you know who was
that was with her?"

"Why, Jerry?"

"Nothing."

"The gentleman whom Miss Middleton is
to marry."

Jerry's countenance changed.

"But what's his name?" he persisted.

"Marley—Mr. Marley."

"And will she marry him in that name?"

"Marry him in that name," I repeated;
"why, what do you mean?"

"Just that, and no more, ma'am dear;
only is that the name he'll take with him to
church?"

"Certainly. Why not?"

"It's a mighty quare crink-um-cranky
world, so it is," observed Jerry, as if he had
neither heard my answer nor my question; and
then, turning to quit the room, he added—
"But I'll find the law and the logic of that
somehow."

"Of what, Jerry?"

"Oh, murder!" he exclaimed, glancing

towards the window; "the game's started, and the hounds in full cry: don't I like to see 'em bothered! Here's the Miss Saunderses, in their Sunday bonnets; and Mrs. Brevet Major's for all the world like a tattered flag-staff. Oh, then, it's kilt intirely, you'll be with the talk of 'em; will I give 'em the law of a bagged fox, and then come round with ₜhe coach to the hall door, and say your honour's carriage is waiting—of course, you'll want the coach: and what I cum to ask you most of all was, I can make meeself fit to go on the coach-box, and no disgrace to you, if I might, and then, maybe, I'd get spaking to her agin, or looking at her, anyhow."

The echoes from my garden-walk told me that Jerry had spoken truly, and that I was exposed to all the horrors of a siege; so I simply said, *he* might do 'as he liked: and while he disappeared out of the back door, the Saunders' and Mrs. Brevet entered at the front. Mrs. Brevet flashed indignation upon me at once. "*Some* people could know every-thing, and make mystery out of what was *no* mystery. It was public enough now—no

thanks to anyone—it was in the papers; and
some who knew it all the time! and then—"

"Private despatches, my dear," interrupted
the major, who had struggled through the
three Misses Saunders, and was swollen to an
unusual size by exercise and anxiety. "Private despatches, eh, my dear friend;" and he
shook me cordially by both hands. "Secret
service! quite right—quite right! Mum!"

"I am sure," spoke the lisping youngest of
the Saunders family, "we should have only
been glad to know for her sake, as Jemima
said, to pay her any little attention: we delighted in her so much; she was such a sweet
little angel! We shall be so happy to call
upon her."

"Ay, ay!" coughed Major Cobb, and then
closed one eye knowingly; "call upon her,
and hear the news, and meet some 'my lords'
and 'my ladies' there, and ask her for orders.
I had you *there*, Miss Sophy: ask her for
orders—gad! I remember once going with
you, my dear, to the gallery."

"Gallery!" shrieked out Mrs. Brevet.
"No; I confess you horrid man, you and

that dear, delightful Giles, who died afterwards at Raoul Pindee, beguiled me once into the pit—I confess *once* to the pit—and I was so agitated, fearing that anyone should recognize me, and that it *might* get round to head-quarters."

"Why Molly," stammered the Major, who, as he grew old, became testy and deaf. "Why Molly, it was the gallery—don't you remember you tried to tie your bonnet to the front rail, and it went over, I remmember it so well, it was a bright red, with golden strings. And there was such a laugh, as it floated away like a scarlet flamingo."

I had not spirits to make a diversion in Mrs. Cobb's favour, though I pitied her, she sat swelling with wounded pride, and indignation, her bitterness by this incident diverted from me, while her husband chuckled and laughed, and rubbed his hands, repeating, "it floated away like a scarlet flamingo—it floated away like a scarlet flamingo."

"Cobb," she exclaimed. "If you go on telling such wicked stories, I'll serve you out, I'll serve you as Borowlasky, the dwarf's wife, serves him. I'll put you on the chimney-piece.

"Floated away—floated away," laughed on the little man, whose memory had conjured up the pleasing picture. "No place like the pit for seeing a play. Suppose we make a snug party, and go to the pit to see little Helen Lyndsey's play. And who would have thought of *your* being in the secret all the time. But, I must say, it serves the Heath people right, they shrunk from the Lyndseys in their time of trouble."

There was a chorus of denying exclamations. " Oh, major! how can you major! "

"Yes, it is all true—and now you will be all ready to run down the poor girl's throat; and take your bothering order-books for autographs. I shan't call on her, no, I *shall not.* I paid her no attention, shewed her no kindness, when I ought to have done so! We all knew their circumstances, and privations. I might have beat up Lyndsey's quarters; kind words enrich the poor, and do not rob the rich; but I gave him none. I shall not call on her, ladies, though I'll go and see her play.

The three Misses Saunders, one and all, not only denied their ever having neglected the Lyndseys; but their ever having neglected anybody else, because of poverty; and they knew the dear major did not mean one word of what he said. Mrs. Brevet persisted in silence; but for the heaving and waving of her feathers, she might have passed, for the wax-work representative of an Imperial family.' The youngest Miss Saunders was considered a saint' by her 'circle.' She never wore a bow in her bonnet, she never curled her hair, she never danced, she never read novels in public, she never went to any place of amusement; nay, she never spoke without an introductory groan, or a soft sigh, and a casting up of the eye, in a mournful lack-a-daisical-way, quite in accordance with her wailing voice. Twice she cleared her throat, and at last said—

"I think it would be only our duty as women, to rally round this leaf cast upon the waters, to prove to the world that she is not deserted by her early friends. It would be worse than unkind to leave a young, lonely

creature as she is, exposed to all the evils and
dangers, the snares and pit-falls of the world,
without one *serious* friend to take her to her
heart, and shew her her danger. I pant to
offer her my friendship, and purpose that we
accompany our friend here to call upon her;
poor sweet lamb!" I begged to decline the
companionship, aud said that Mr. Lyndsey's
health was so precarious, that Miss Lyndsey
at yet, could not receive visitors.

"But she has sent for the youngest Ryland,"
said the eldest Saunders—"sent for her to be
with her at twenty-one minutes past nine this
morning. Miss Lyndsey must have the strength
of an elephant to endure that after last night
—they let that out to Mrs. Bruce's lady's-
maid, and then had the impudence to refuse
Mrs. Bruce Miss Lyndsey's address—gave
themselves such airs—although Mrs. Bruce
asked it as a favour—said that, as Miss Helen
trusted them, they *could* not. I wonder will
Miss Helen permit them to make her dresses,
now she has become—we hardly know how—
a fine rich lady."

"Noble Helen—noble Helen!" repeated

the major, who was never prone to attend to what Miss Saunders said—" noble girl! fit to command—worthy to command—a regiment. She has led a forlorn hope, and triumphed; paying off her father's debts by the sweat of her brain."

" Brow, you mean, I suppose," shouted Mrs. Brevet.

" No, ma'am, I mean *brain*; I mean what I say, Mrs. Cobb, and am quite able to say what I mean,"—and the irate major beat his foot in a merciless manner upon my hearth-rug.

" You are not married," suggested Mrs. Cobb, *sotto voce*, to Miss Saunders, and attempting to look like a martyr. Miss Saunders shrugged her shoulder-bones.

" At all events," said the youngest fair one, " our friend will give Miss Lyndsey's address, and we can write."

I could *not* give such an address, and, therefore, declined in the most civil manner possible, saying I was not at liberty to do so for a few days; but that did not save me.

" Oh, very well, madam !" exclaimed Mrs. Brevet Major, rising, and shaking herself like a roused lion, throwing at the same time a look of annihilation at her husband ; " you wish to keep the star to yourself, as you have always done—every creature on the heath is talking of it—but I can tell you that *won't do now*— every soul in England would rise in arms against such a monopoly—of course, it has answered your purpose to be mysterious, and ——."

Jerry entered with a flourish and announced the carriage; the Misses Saunders took alarm at the lady's vehemence, and rapidly wished me good morning; the major, whose deafness prevented his hearing *all* she said, became wrathful at what he did hear, without understanding it, and stamped, and uttered bits of honest kindness and sound wisdom which had nothing to do with the immediate subject; while his wife blustered—about unneighbourly neighbours, the consideration she had been accustomed to receive, the various confidences reposed in her, her fitness for all the duties of life, collectively and in the abstract—her in-

fluence at head-quarters, and her determination
to storm the theatre, discover Helen Lyndsey's
'ambush,' constitute herself her chaperone (provided her previous conduct merited her patronage), and introduce her to the fashionable
world! which, she added, emphatically, must
be done by a 'Somebody,' not a 'NOBODY.'

Just as she concluded this tirade, I heard
Jerry's full round brogue giving vent to exclamations and prayers, that could have but
one object; and, in a moment, Helen grasped
my hand affectionately in hers. I did not see
that the Misses Saunders followed her into the
room, or that Mrs. Brevet shrunk quivering
into a corner, or that the little Major involun-
tarily raised his finger, as if saluting a superior
officer—we must have formed a strange picture,
while she was kissing me, foreign fashion, on
both cheeks. She comprehended at a glance
who were present, and, with the tact that cannot be taught or described, was at ease with
them, and placed them on the best footing with
themselves, at once. She rejoiced to see Mrs.
Cobb looking so well; and her old friend, the
major, did he remember how he saved Finette

from the butcher's dog? With much real feeling, the old man kissed her hand, and, with the genuine honesty of his nature, told her it was more than kind to remember the one act of civility he had shown her. The Misses Saunders puzzled her a little; she did not know which was which. The youngest made as if she desired to embrace her, and then drew back, with the shyness of affectation; all putting on that peculiar air of diffidence and admiration, aided by a shrug, a stare, and a whisper, which the small-minded and ignorant imagine to be the proper manner towards 'an authoress.' It was quite impossible to discover what Helen thought of this. She talked, she smiled, she jested—she was as perfectly at home with them as if she had never been separated, as if she had been their cherished friend, all her life long; she listened to Mrs. Brevet's flourishes with a complacency so perfect, that the poor lady saw herself in the glass of her very vivid imagination, acting as pioneer or drill-major to 'the talented young authoress,' amid the *élite* of London society. She resolved to 'take up'

the young *crayshur* (this word was always one
of her suspicious pronunciations), and dress
her like the *Corinne* of Madame de Staël. She
sunned her in the longest and broadest smiles,
and cast upon me the most withering glances
of triumph and contempt. I was annoyed at
Helen's bearing this, and felt myself growing
sulky. She accepted a tract from the youngest Miss Saunders, and even seemed interested
in what that little mincing fool called 'her
dream,' for discovering, what Jerry afterwards
explained to me 'was an uninhabited island,
where she might convert the heathens that lived
there.' She inquired after that abominable
Mrs. Bruce, and instead of standing up bravely
in defence of Miss Ryland's merits as a dress-
maker, she listened and laughed, until Mrs.
Brevet nodded her head in a most impertinent
manner, as well as to say, "I think we have
done for Miss Ryland." The major, I saw, was
fairly bewitched by her. She threw her net-
work over them all, as dexterously as a gossamer spider casts his threads over a bunch of
hawthorn, and which are only discovered by
the diamonds of dew that glitter upon them.

She parried their inquiries after her where-
abouts with so much tact, that, with all their
curiosity they conceived themselves complimented by not being told where she lived—
just yet."

Once only her eyes flashed; it was at
some coarse allusion made by Mrs. Brevet,
to the unhappy differences between her
parents. She rose, as a young eagle soars
above the valley he scorns, and Mrs. Brevet
quailed before her. The poor major *saw* the
mistake, though he did not hear the words,
and made matters worse by his repeated enquiries of "what's that? what's that?" Helen
was the first to change from the eagle into the
dove, and turn off his wife's mistake with a
smile and a compliment. I was astonished,
but not pleased.—She had more tact than
I believed consistent with the honesty
which one human being owes another in all
the relations of life. Mrs. Brevet, with ori-
ental magnificence, placed her carriage, her
house, her husband at her disposal, and suggested that 'her talent' should not go about
in a hired coach. I saw scorn quivering on

Helen's lip, and hoped it would speak, but it only quivered and remained silent, declining the offer with a curtsey, which was almost as gratifying as acceptance. The company seemed inclined to stay her out, when, saying she had come to run away with her own dear 'NOBODY,' the major turned round, gave his military salute, and exclaimed in a commanding tone, " *Quick march !* " upon which, with a renewal of offers and protestations, and Miss Saunders, junior, passing another tract into Helen's hand, with a proud casting up of her eloquent eyes, the company withdrew; Helen saving me all trouble, by accompanying them to the door, adieuing and smiling until they were shut out by Jerry, who muttered—

"Bad cess to them all but the ould gentleman, for a set of hippocrites ! do they think people have no memories in their heads, and no feeling in their hearts ? And to see you, Miss Helen, darling, throwing your pearls before swine, wasting your smiles upon such a bundle of bewilderment as the whole of them —it's the could shoulder I'd have given *them,* as well as everyone else on the Heath, barring

the poor Rylands.   Sure it isn't *natural* to
harbour those who never ask who you are, but
what you have.   No wonder my head's grey
with the decaitfulness of the *univarse*."

CHAPTER VI.

"Does Time, with his cold wing wither,
Each feeling that once was dear?
Then, child of misfortune, come hither,
I'll weep with thee, tear for tear."

MOORE.

———

"HAVE you seen Florence, to-day,"questioned Helen, abruptly, after dismissing Jerry with a few brief but kind words, which he so well knew how to appreciate.

"No, my dear, I have not; I have not left Hampstead to-day." I was a little put out by the question. She must have known I could not have been in town; but she con-continued without seeming to observe it:—

"I asked Marley to take me to her, and he

neither refused, nor promised to do so. I would not ask a second time, but went by myself."

"When?"

"This morning: I was there before she left her dressing-room, and astonished her and her maid by entering. Now tell me ———"

And she drew the very chair she used to sit on when a child, opposite to where I sat, and, leaning forward, took both my hands in hers, and fixed her eyes steadily upon mine. Such a searching, in-looking gaze as it was! I wondered what she could see in my great, round hazel eyes to look at. I do not know anything so seriously uncomfortable as that species of scrutiny which seems to doubt your truth, and keeps looking for flaws in your character, in a manner the most determined. I do not think I should have borne it from anyone but Helen. At last, grasping my hands, so that my fingers tingled, she inquired—

"Is Florence really in spirit—in soul—what she seems to be?"

"What an extraordinary question!"

"I repeat it:—Is she in spirit and in soul what she seems to be? Think!"

"Think!" I repeated, bewildered by her manner and question.

"You are not thinking," she exclaimed, impatiently; "or if you are, you are wondering in your simple thought why I should question the truth of your immaculate Florence."

I was offended, and she saw it.

"Believe me, I shall not love her the more from finding how she rivals me—yes, rivals me—in your affection."

"Helen, Helen, I do not know you at times."

"At times!" she repeated. "You might have known me once," and her voice sank into so mournful a tone, that I could have wept; "you might have known me *once*—if I ever was simple and innocent as a child ought to be—for like seeks like—and despite all that people philosophise about the harmony of opposites, I do not believe in *that*, any more than in many other things; but as I say, you might have known me then—but now!—you

have *vegetated*, I have *lived*—lived!—and such
a life—every feeling corroded, hardened, petri-
fied by circumstances; but that is not what I
wanted to say—and there now, *you* are thinking—you are trying, as in *lang syne*, to make
everything I say fit in, as if it were Mosaic; to
take off my corners—to set me on the old
pedestal you fixed for me years ago, when no
one but you and the seamstress believed in
me. But never mind that—is Florence heart
and soul, bright pure nature?—is she what
she *seems?*—is it really the light of a true unsullied nature that beams in her eyes?—is she
the actual, the real, the unselfish womanly
creature she looks—with but little less of
beauty and goodness than the angels that do
homage before the throne of God!"

"Yes, I know that Florence is all she
seems; you have understood her, and you
have done her justice."

Her eyes fell, and she relaxed her grasp of
my hands, while her own sank listlessly by her
side, and her voice faltered into a whisper—

"No, if she is what she seems, it is not
given to such as I am, to do her justice—you,

dear NOBODY, in the strength of your simplicity, in the faithful, believing innocence of your heart, render her more actual justice than I *could* do, were I to pour forth whole volumes in her praise. May God keep to you for ever your simple, child-like faith in human virtue—may it sit by your bed of death as a crowning reality.—I know what it is to go through the world betrayed and deceived, until faith becomes a ghastly skeleton instead of a living presence. God keep your faith, human and divine, green in your soul—God keep it to you, and may you always believe—in Florence!"

"And in you, dearest Helen."

"Believe in me! well, yes, to a certain extent. I shall not be displeased if you believe in me. I wish I felt that you *ought* to do so. But about Florence; she interested me so much this morning, that I have quite forgotten my popularity, and how I enjoyed the idea of everybody being at fault, and not knowing where to find me. The tone of knowledge and mystery of the morning papers is most amusing. One declares that the identity of 'H. L.' has been known to them from

the first moment, when the first poem appeared
in a certain journal; another assumes that I am
not myself, but a multiplature, a sort of literary
Hydra, writing with the same pen and ink;
another—and another—another;—all but
one professes to be well informed as to who I
am, declares that no woman could have written
the more philosophic portions of the drama,
the report that a *young* lady is the author, being too absurd to need contradiction, as the
least practised critic must know that the frame-
work of the play is constructed by a master
hand.   Marley told me, that old Lady C——
was at the door of the theatre this morning
at eight, before the poor hacks were on duty,
to learn my address, to secure me, of course,
for her next conversazione! Ah! do
you remember at my entreaty, our once
waiting at *her* door, when moonlight and lamp-
light mingled together, to see Lord Byron
go in, and my rushing to touch his coat, and
then it was *not* Lord Byron after all! and my
crying all the way back, and your buying a
great cake to comfort me!"

Yes, of course, I remembered it all—
everything. What had I ever forgotten connected with her! but I reverted to Florence
—why should Marley resolve to keep these
young persons apart? "Let me," I said,
"dearest Helen, let me say one word of
Florence."

"Another time, to-morrow, or the day after,
we will talk of her. I have only, dear friend, to
remember what I, myself, am, and then to remember what you think me. Now these two
memories combined—lead to the conclusion,
that where your affections are concerned, your
judgments are not always the most correct.
So I will see a little more of Florence before I
determine."

"Determine what?"

"What I determine," she replied, nervously,
rolling and unrolling the riband of her bonnet.
"But I will not be questioned, what I wish to
say, I say, what I desire to conceal—torture,
or what people consider worse than torture—
death! could not wring from me. Let us
leave Florence for the present to herself, for
me, I have a *rôle* to play—and will play it out.

The drama—which the papers say has had a triumph, and must have a run—will give me wealth, for my wants are few, whatever my wishes may be—and what I have dreamed of, worked for—fame! I long to prove what the homage born of fame will do for me, in the way of happiness—mind, I expect nothing! I try an experiment, that is all; the path of duty has been thickly set with thorns; were my father sane—his love and delight might have made me happy; though I am so hedged in by circumstances, I cannot tell—! This very morning when daylight was struggling to penetrate the atmosphere, and the poor lark I told you of, was quivering in its cage—fluttering over the dusty turf, which, perhaps, even its imagination converted into a 'fragrant shrine,'—even then, after the fearful excitement of my play, I blessed God that my father's mental vision was gone—that he had eyes that saw not, ears that heard not."

"But how could this be, Helen!"

"How! well, I cannot tell you yet—perhaps, I may never live to tell you—!"

"I must say," I exclaimed, urging on

words, which I had not courage to think over,
for, I confess, I was a little afraid of Helen—
perhaps fear is *not* the word—I did not like to
excite her—and I wanted her to love me,
without seeking perhaps to inspire what would
have given her confidence in my opinions—"I
must say I should like to know all *you* know
of Marley; and I cannot but add, dear Helen,
that, knowing his engagement with Florence,
it was a little imprudent of you to leave the
theatre with him alone; and more, you have
seen him this morning!"

The bolt thus shot, I wished myself any-
where but where I was. I expected an angry
declaration of her right to do as she pleased,
and was quite astonished at the look of innocent surprise which stole over her features—
this was followed by one of her soft, musical
laughs.

"Why, this *is* good!—but to be sure you
do not know. Is my lot, then, so cast, that
even you cannot believe in me?—why is fate
so at war with me, that I dare not be frank
even to you? alas!—no wonder my play should
be successful, when I give the fiction to the

world, and my own life is the reality! I cannot tell you *now* what I know of Marley,
perhaps I may never tell you. Florence
jealous of me!—heaven bless her!—if she
married Marley, she would be ———" She
stopped abruptly; and, while her face faded
into the most delicate pallor—"there is no
need to call upon our imagination for the
great events, or, indeed, the small events, of
life," she added; "but never again speak to
me of Marley—doubt me in any way you
please, but do not speak of *him*."

"But, my dearest Helen, others will speak
of him; you may be *sans peur*, but unless you
are careful, you cannot continue *sans reproche*,
particularly *now*, when your glories will be set
on high for 'daws to peck at.'"

"All is true that you have said, or can
say," she answered; "but my own friend must
excuse my giving an explanation *now*. I am
going to take lodgings at Brompton."

"At Brompton!" I exclaimed; "but why
go so far out of the world as that? who can
get at you in that unchanged district, inter-
sected with lanes and lawns, and ditches,

where Cromwell and Mrs. Fitzherbert, and
Burleigh and Billington rusticated? They
will take you for a soprano or contralto seeking retirement!"

"Very well, indeed, for *you*, dear NOBODY; but
I can get soft air and the retirement so bene-
ficial to my father, and soft fresh air so necessary to me what people call a healthy, bracing
air, irritates me beyond endurance. I shall
not be ashamed of my address."

She was urging me to return to town with
her, to see her new domicile, when Jerry, who
never thought it requisite to inquire if I could
see him, tapped at the door, and, without
waiting, opened it: he always came into a
room head foremost, cautiously dragging the
remainder of his body in by easy stages.

"I'm proud to see ye together, ladies.
When the coast was clear, I sent the coach
back, and yet *that* couldn't be done *unknownst*
to the heath. 'Then Miss Lyndsey stops the
day at the cottage,' says Miss Saunders, way-
laying me—the miserable looking one, whose
religion does not seem to agree with her—
and quite a mob gathered round the pump,

just to learn from me when they could get a sight of you; and two things I wanted, Miss Helen."

He laid on the table, what seemed to me, a square box, which he carried in his hand; it was carefully tied up in a handkerchief, so that its contents were a mystery; and then advancing to where Helen sat, he fell down on his knees before her, clasping tightly his embrowned hands, which were strained and knotty, and every muscle in his eloquent face working—

"First and foremost, ma'am, the master; I hear he's not strong and hearty in himself, weak-like and failing; he's not ould, Miss Helen—not near as much fallen into years as myself—but there's no accounting for the sickness. Oh, Miss Helen, darlint! for the sake of ould times—for the sake of the dear ould times—sopped, as they war, in sorrow, just keep list'ning to me, not so much with your *ears*, as with your *heart*; and, darling, even then you know the comfort the master took out of me—me that tended him, and the horses, dear, giving them their oats to the last grain, watching to their shoeing, grooming, physicking, and studying them with all the eyes in my head, day and night; valeting them (the master, I mean), and tending his clothes, and many a time the ould cook would settle her cap at his boots—they had such a polish!—and always clip and singed him with my own hands, until every jockey said there wasn't such a cob on the common; and now, Miss Helen, if you'll let me go back to the masther, I'll tend him day and night on my four bones, and want no wages, nor trouble the house for a bit or a sup—for I can ate or drink any-thing, or do without it. I know *you* don't think anything about that, only the English servants, dear, don't like us, we do with so little; so I want to show it's not a throuble I'd be. And the masther! oh, only let me get a sight of him, and I'll tend him as if he was a new-born babby. Do, Miss Helen, look! if he don't take to me in one hour, I'll never ask ye a second time, I won't indeed! I know it would brake all the heart that's left in me, but never mind, if he don't take to me, as he used, I'll never ask to stay. Oh, say I

may, Miss Helen, jewel, say I may; I know
what ails him better than anyone; for the
love of mercy let your poor Jerry have that
much consolation. I know what ails him; I
know what runs in the blood of the family; I
could do him so much good. Don't turn from
me, Miss Helen; look down upon me, as you
hope to have mercy yourself."

"That will do, Jerry, that will do; I cannot
bear it. Yes, you shall see my father, he was
much attached to you, and when we were
abroad, before he became so very ill, he often
spoke of you."

"He did, did he!" exclaimed Jerry—"hear
that, now!—I thought as much. Oh, Miss
Helen, if you had thrusted *me* that night,
sure it's to the ends of the *earth* I'd have gone
with you and the masther, and no one the
wiser. The dear masther! he knows, and
knows well, that I can keep a sacret. 'My
poor Jerry,' he says to me, 'you're thrue and
as silent as night;' and I'll make myself look
as like myself as ever I can, and tune up my
bits of songs, and I may bring him back, who
can tell?"

"How did you know he was gone *that way* ?" enquired Helen, breathlessly.

" What other way would he be gone !"

" You shall see him," said Helen, with forced calmness ; " but suppose you cannot serve him ?"

" And what will hinder me ? didn't I sarve him long ?"

" I mean, suppose you do him no good ?"

" Ah ! don't be looking into the darkness, dear. Where's the use of it ? There's only one darkness we should ever think of, and that has a bright light *beyond it*. It *will* do him good. Sure, it can do him no harm to thry."

" Very well, Jerry ; you shall see him."

Jerry poured out thanks and blessings, but Helen had fallen into a fit of musing, and did not hear him. At last, he exclaimed—

" Miss Helen, dear, come back to yourself ; come back, dear, and listen. What do you think I've got in my handkecher ?"

" I can't tell, Jerry."

" No, you can't, miss ; you'd never think of it."

" A model of old Staggers?" and she forced
a laugh.

" No, miss; I never took any pride out of
Staggers; he was a poor, mean-spirited ani-
mal—never did me a bit of credit; no, dear.
But what do you think of—the—starling?"

"What! Bright-eye—Bob Bright-eye!—my
own bird! Oh, Jerry!" Pleasure flushed her
cheeks, while she sprang at the handkerchief,
and hastily undid the knots. It fell from off
the cage, and there, immovable as the wooden
perch on which he stood, was poor Bob—that
is to say, his dusty feathers—stiff and stark,
and large projecting glass-bead eyes, to re-
place those so full of lustre.

The instantaneous change that passed over
Helen's face was most painful; the expression
changed from intense pleasure to disappointment and disgust; she became quite pale, and
her lips quivered; she clenched her hands,
and stamped with childish violence.

" Oh, why did you so!" she exclaimed—
"why did you this!—why bring me this
mockery of life—I thought I should have my
bird again! In a moment it was before me;

his quaint head on one side, his soft, quick eyes, and his clear, sharp voice—life—life pulsing in every feather. Not this dim, dull, rusty, senseless lump—shapeless, too! —my poor, graceful bird! to mangle your delicate flesh, and wrench your sinews, and puff you out—oh, it was cruel! Jerry, why could you not let the dead rest? A little sod would have covered his remains—a little green sod—and the swallows would dash over it, and, it might be, the redbreast rest his slender legs upon the turf, and lament his 'passing away;' but to see my poor bird thus!—so dim and dreary—such a mockery of life! I saw once abroad a little maid who was drowned, and they dressed her, in her coffin, as if for a fête—they painted her cheeks, and crossed her white, waxy hands over her guitar —it was horrible!—this bird is almost as sad! Take it away, Jerry, you have given me much pain."

The poor fellow covered up the unlucky cage, and shambled with it towards the door. My heart ached for him; for I saw how he had wished to preserve the bird, thinking it would give Helen pleasure, and not grief.

"Miss Helen," I said, "knows you did this with the kindest intention, only you did not understand her; she could not bear to see dead what she had so much loved alive."

"May God help her then," he replied, while his poor eyes overflowed—"may God help her! for it's what we're all born to look at, some time or other; and it's awful and grand, the stillness and the silence of what was once so full of the spirit and glory of the Lord; but this little bird had nothing to do with that; I had it done, and kept it for her in the bottom of my box, and left a bit of a note, ma'am, for you on the top of it, in case I was called of a sudden, just to ax you to give it her. I'd rather tear my heart out than vex her; but it's often so; I'm an unfortunate ould sinner; and the sooner the world's shut of me the better. I'm ever maning right, and doing wrong; it's hard upon me—so it is—to be so unfortunate. I often thought I'd yet another bird instead of Bob Bright-eye, for all of his kind are as like each other as twin shamrocks; and just as I have heard tell, that a king never dies, because there's one always ready and willing to pop into his place, so I could have a Bob

Bright-eye always to the fore, and thought of it; but again, sure, setting a case, that it was *a* starling, it wouldn't be *the* starling, no more than our King George, God bless him! though quite a king, would be all as one as that murdering King Harry the Eighth, who, they say, massacreed seven wives, and the holy Pope of Rome; turn it which way I could, if I had done it, I could make nothing but a lie out o' it, and so I thought I'd just let it alone; and as I'd nothing to stuff meeself, I thought I'd just stuff the bird; and, after all, see what's come of it!"

Is it not singular, how such a mistake as that which Jerry made, will produce a wound hard to cure, and how a memory of former service is lost, by what is only a kindness out of tune! I found it hard to prevail on her to let Jerry see her father; indeed, had she not given her promise, it would have been next to impossible to bring her round.

CHAPTER VI.

"Man, to the last, is but a froward child,
So eager for the future, come what may,
And to the present so insensible."

ROGERS.

———

POOR Jerry waited at the door, but Helen was
so irritable and impatient, that I felt I dared
not urge her to admit him *then;* the poor
fellow was trembling with eagerness and fear;
people always said, that 'the merest trifle
would put Helen out;' but we are above all
things ill-judges of what are trifles to each
other; the 'trifle' to the clear-headed man of
business, is a fearful perplexity to the person
who has neither business comprehension nor

I 2

habits; the 'trifle' to the rich man, is the impossibility of the poor one; the 'trifle' to the indifferent, is the agony of the lover or the friend; the 'trifle' to the unprincipled, causes the honest man to shudder; the servant's 'trifle' would be the fair lady's fatigue; the farmer's 'trifle' would fag out a dozen of our frail and feeble men of fashion; a postponed 'trifle' would cause the blush of shame to overspread the features of an independent fellow, who would have paid if he could; while a hecatomb of 'trifles' would be nothing to the unprincipled man of fashion or folly, who neither knew nor cared what sufferings the creditor endured!

Truly, how much do we require the perfection of that charity ' which thinketh no evil'—— what great need we all have to measure our neighbour's corn by our neighbour's bushel, and not by our own!——how much need for the small coin of daily kindness; how bitterly we complain of the harsh judgments we experience, and how little are we prone to consider the harsh judgments we enter against others. I could have rated Helen Lyndsey at that moment for her injustice, quite forgetting the nervous and highly-wrought temperament which exaggerated every feeling — every suffering—every affection—and was equally prone to exaggerate her own faults. If she had not looked directly into Jerry's face, she might have nursed her anger, for at least a mile; but, when I saw her eyes fixed upon that rugged mingling of the ugliest features with the most earnest and benevolent expression that ever warmed an honest face, I knew that her better nature was in the ascendant; her brow rapidly expanded and cleared, the flush of outraged feeling faded from her cheeks, her eyes no longer flashed, but beamed with all a woman's gentleness; and her lips parted with that peculiar smile, so expressive of sympathy and sweetness, that its very memory is a blessing. She held out her little hand to the old servant. "Why, then, the Lord look down upon you?" he exclaimed. "Sure it's proud I'd be to have ye murder me, every

day of the year, just to have one of them
smiles bring me to life again ! and will I come
Miss Helen dear ? and will I see the dear
gentleman ? thank you, Miss Helen, and long
life to you; I'm a man till the day of my death,
I am—the sooner I die the better, for fear
my luck would turn.   To-morrow ! thank
you darlin—to-morrow ? sure I'll think it a
year till then, and when I'm in it, day and
night will be all one to Jerry !"

" It is impossible to imagine how long
this eloquence might have continued, had
not Helen bounded into the carriage, and
rolled herself up like a little puss in the
corner.   When relieved of Jerry's presence,
it was evident to me that the remembrance
of the dead bird, crushed her as much as
an actual calamity—the loss of a friend or
relative—would have crushed a less imagina-
tive person.   She did not speak a word,
her eyes seemed double their usual size, and
the pupils dilated and contracted, as she
stared straight out of the window.   At last

their expression softened, and a flood of tears
rushed to her relief. "What a cold selfish
creature I have been, and how I *hate* myself,"
she exclaimed, "how could I behave as
I have done? the poor faithful fellow, starving himself to preserve that dead bird—
thinking of me—keeping it for me—judging,
as people always do, that what would
give him pleasure, must give *me* pleasure.
But I forgot the lapse of years—forgot that
Bob was a very old bird when I left him—
forgot all about him, and, like an idiot, fancied my bird, bright as ever, beneath that
handkerchief! A record of my sensations would
fill a volume; I never felt more bitterly disappointed; and how unworthy of me, to turn
upon that faithful fool! It is just possible
that my father may awake somewhat at the
sound of his voice, for he really loved Jerry.
There was—there must have been some bond
between them the nature of which *I* never
knew."

At last, by placing new ideas before her, I

led her to set that one idea aside; gradually she talked of other things; though, as I have said, I had a trying time of it—not that I minded what is called 'trouble,' as people are wont to call pains-taking; those who make trouble of pains-taking for *friends*, are not worthy to have them to take pains for. But Helen treated me as a child—told me just what she liked. There are some people of so inquisitive a nature, that they seek to discover their neighbours' concerns with as much avidity and interest as if they cared for them. They smell a secret, as a pointer scents a covey, and start it whirling through the world with as much glee. My desire to discover what connection existed between Helen and Marley, was not curiosity; but I would as soon have thought of robbing Helen of her purse, as of her secret. There is but one way of honoura-bly learning what you desire to know, and that is by a direct question—open-eyed, straight-forward. I knew she was fond both of mys-tery and of tormenting those she loved;

but, poor thing! she was sorely tried. Still,
I did rejoice when that day was over,
and I left her comfortably lodged in what
if standing now, must be a very old-
fashioned house — for then it was anything
but new; but I fear it has been swept off by
that destroyer of all that is old or hallowed—
the 'Modern Improvement Society;' that
would as soon pull down a cathedral as look
at it—though it had been consecrated to God
by God's ministers, and sheltered the ashes of
a thousand kings—if it stood in the way of a
steam-engine, or a patent bone-boiling company! I solemnly declare, as an honourable
gentlewoman who never willingly told a lie in
her life, and never slept on a misrepresen-
tation without correcting it before she laid her
head on her pillow, that I do not know England. It seems to me, particularly in a drawing-room full of 'New Englanders,' that I
have got into a strange country, where all is
un-English except the language; even that
has

   " Suffered a sea change."

For instance, no one ever hears now-a-days of
a 'dissipated' young man; but a 'fast' young
man is, I suspect, one and the same thing.
We never heard of a 'dissipated young lady;'
but I have, to my womanly shame, encoun-
tered well-educated, well-connected, young
females—'ladies,' at all events, by courtesy,
who wear jaunty hats, jackets with coachmen's
buttons, and absolutely call their father
'governor,' and their mother 'old lady.' I
suspect they must be in some way connected
with a new sect, of which I know little, but
hear a great deal—'Strong-minded women!'
So busied is this particular sect about real or
imaginary grievances—so eager to overturn
the laws of God, and to make a new position
for themselves—so busy about certain 'rights,'
as to become quite oblivious of certain duties;
in fact, strange as it seems, they desire to be
considered *men* in all things except their responsibilities. I have not, however, heard how
they intend to dispose of the marital question,
or the duties of maternity. The age is *anti-*

reverential in all things, and yet numbers who
are carried along by the sweeping current of
novelty, which, however it may be turned,
never leaves things exactly as it found
them, seek to raise the new to the level of the
old, and have no desire to pull down or to
destroy the great and the beautiful. Yet,
so insidious is innovation, that old things *are*
destroyed. Old trees in that very district of
Old Brompton have been remorselessly up-
rooted, though hallowed by the tradition that
they were planted by hands dear to our country; and houses, whose every stone was a
history, have now neither a 'local habitation
nor a name,' except in the church-books of
the parish of Kensington! A passion is growing upon us for wide streets and wide roads
(we are become as extensive in our ideas as if
ours was not a small island), and the consequence is, that some of our streets look as
dreary as those I have heard of at Munich,
and that without the dignity so necessary to
carry off size. I mourn over the landmarks

of history as I would over the deaths of friends.
I quite dread wandering into my old haunts,
lest I should find my early homes obliterated,
and that light bright lath-and-plaster " villas,"
all plate glass and green paint—have taken
their places.

It was a square brick dwelling, with
a tiled roof, nearly covered by gigantic
climbers, roses run to wood, sacrificing their
beauty to their ambition, and clematis, matted
and self-willed, towering over the gable—a
very snow-storm in the season. This quaint
house was surrounded by high brick walls,
that overshadowed a lawn, bordered by ancient
evergreens, and where periwinkle, Aaron's-
beard, all heights and hues of half-weed
flowers, and stalky wall-flowers, seemed to
grow, without caring or being cared for; snap-
dragon, also, but small, and stunted, and
tufted dandelion, and abundant stone-crop,
maiden-hair, and two or three clumps of harts-
tongue fern sprouted from the walls, and relieved the monotony of the grey, or short,

dark-green velvet moss, which coated them
as with an old and time-honoured garment. A
dial was set up where the sun never shone;
nothing could have looked more miserable
and deserted: and in the opposite corner
stood a pump, with pretensions to taste;
for an old gurgoile was converted into a
spout, and the column was surmounted by a
carved cap, like a helmet. I did not admire
it; but it was old and quaint, and stood
beneath a Rowan tree, recalling the old
rhyme—

> " The spring beneath the rowan tree
> Is the sweetest that can be."

I doubt if a 'spring' had selected that pump
for its mouth-piece; for, peeping into a rent in
the wall just behind, I saw a number of
dormant snails clinging round a leaden pipe,
which was powerfully suggestive of Chelsea
Water-works. For all that, it looked pic-
turesque in the corner; a banner of gigantic ivy rustling above it, while within the ever-
green sanctuary nestled a large colony of

chattering sparrows; the lawn itself was charming, and so was an old mulberry tree, nearly in
its centre, one of those planted by James the
First, who paid the soft air of Brompton the
compliment of thinking it qualified the district to become a mulberry garden; one of
the walls flanked Love Lane, which straggled
between sweet solid hedges of white-thorn, on
to Kensington.   Helen was as enchanted with
it, as if it had been a palace; she carried a
chair out from the entrance for her father to sit
on, and rolled her cloak to place beneath his
feet, all under the mulberry tree.   Poor man!
his head generally rested on his breast; but
it seemed as if that delicious air revived
him; he leaned back, looked round, called
Helen, and knew her when she came, and
evinced the most childish delight as she
gathered him some flowers.

"He may recover!—he may recover!"—she
repeated, in ecstacy, and the same moment
shuddered while she murmured—"yet why
should I desire *that;* rather, God forbid!"

But still volatile and unresting, her buoyant spirits rejoiced in the aspect and foliage of what, from its high walls, appeared to me akin to a prison. From what I have written, I daresay the 'Modern Improvement Society' will wonder why I could wish it to remain. Alas! they know little, and care less, about the heart's stronghold—' association.'

Helen knew so little about the rooms they were to occupy, that I asked her how it happened she was so ignorant. I hope my excessive fatigue and weariness of spirit did not make me unjust to her; but I fancied she turned upon me with a mischievous and pleased knowledge that the communication she was about to make would teaze me.

"I never saw the place before Marley fixed upon it!"

How I hated myself for finding it hard to believe in her! and yet, after an hour, during my drive home, the faith returned. Oh, the unspeakable strength which springs up as faith in our kind increases—how it elevates ourselves: nothing draws us downward deeper or with greater certainty than an unbelieving nature!

When I entered my little drawing-room, the table was covered with cards, notes, and letters; notes in those days were hand-delivered, and letters, solid bath-post affairs, not fastened with a splash of gum-water, and what looks, at best, like a device for printed muslin, but a heavy seal, and the greater the quantity of wax expended, the greater the respect evinced for the person addressed. Some of the seals I broke after my return were as large as a five-shilling piece; but *I do* think the manager's was largest of all; such entreaties that *we* would go to the theatre that night, he had promised my lord this, and my lady that, and so and so, to name them to H. L.; in short, the whole town 'was at her feet!' would she command his services, would she permit him the honour of waiting upon her, would I kindly intercede that he might have that gratification!"

I sat down to try to think calmly over the past, and to speculate as to the future, but I could make nothing of it. I knew she would absolutely rejôice in the manager's disappointment, and exult in his having been drawn into unauthorized promises of introduction; he was judging her by the usual standard of those who believe notoriety to be fame, and enjoy the one as much as the other. Helen knew the value and the price of both, and if she had achieved a throne, I question whether she would not make her subjects tremble.

CHAPTER VII.

"These are the spiders of society;
  They weave their petty web of lies and sneers,
  And lie themselves in ambush for the spoil."

A VERY large letter—larger than even the manager's missive—sealed with the undoubted Cobb coat of arms ! And about that said coat of arms, there was a story—how, not liking the original ' coat ' appertaining to the Cobb family (which, indeed, there had been much difficulty in finding, if it ever was really *found* at all) Mrs. Brevet instructed an artist to add sundry imaginings of her own ; so that, how-

ever incongruous as a whole, the Cobb coat
was as large as that of the Duke of Norfolk.
There was no such seal in the neighbourhood;
and it was only used on special occasions.

As the style of invitation contained in that
letter, is now matter of polite history, I
transcribe it for the benefit of the present
generation:

"Major and Mrs. Brevet Major Cobb present their compliments to Mistress Susan ——,
and request the honour of her company to
dinner, on Tuesday, the eleventh of ——,
18—, at five o'clock punctually, to meet the
celebrated 'H. L——.' Miss Helen Lyndsey.

"The favour of an immediate answer is
requested."

An invitation to dine at the Cobb's! there
was an event in my uneventful life! Had it
not been for the fresh tide of circumstances,
which lately poured upon me, I dare say I
should have been driven into the extravagance
of a new dress; but, as it was, I had nothing
to think of in that way. Mrs. Cobb asked no

householders to dinner, who did not give
dinners in return, and, as I never invited anyone, except to an early tea (half-past five),
and a frugal ten o'clock supper, this was the
first time I had been so honoured. I felt
inclined to be high-minded, and decline, but I
was curious to see how Helen would be received there, and determined to make one
of the party; perhaps, also, I should not have
liked to have been left out. If Buonaparte
(we never called him Napoleon then—indeed,
he was generally called Boney)—if Buonaparte had effected a landing beside the great
pond in the Vale, it could hardly have created
a greater sensation than this much-talked-of
dinner. Everybody visited everybody; there
was a perpetual current of people up the hill
and down the hill, and over the heath; those
who were so happy as to have received invitations to the dinner, or even for an hour in
the evening, looked down with contempt on
the non-invited; the women adopted every
possible organ of investigation to discover

what Mrs. or Miss So-and-so intended to
wear; 'Ackerman's fashions' never were in
such demand, and there was a never-ending,
still-beginning, palpitating, little crowd around
Miss Ryland's door all day long. Mrs. Brevet
had roundly told the Misses Saunders that she
expected all her visitors to come in new
dresses; and this intelligence—added to the
propensity which all have, in a greater or less
degree, to purchase, try on, and finally display
a 'new dress'—sent our ladies, day after day,
to town, to decide and arrange their finery.
Helen declared she traced the Saunders's down
one side of Bond Street, and up the other,
whenever she drove that way : they tried hard
to discover what Mrs. Brevet herself intended
to wear; but Mrs. B. was, as she said herself,
'bomb-proof,' and invariably replied, "Wait,
and see." The exulting and triumphant look,
which accompanied this impressive mandate,
led to a report that the 'major's lady' was to
be arrayed in a vest of cloth of gold, wearing a
shawl presented by the Rajah of some 'Pore'

or other, à la Pasta, and a flame-coloured
turban, with a bird-of-paradise plume.

The pious Miss Saunders shed tears at this
report. "A woman," she said, "at that poor
dear, benighted Mrs. Brevet Major Cobb's
time of life, yielding to such vanities, and
dressing in such a way, as to outshine everyone! in her own house, too—such bad taste!
Who could dress up to all them Indian things?
she would like to know. *She* had no wish to
do so—heaven knows! A pure-white muslin,
with a little extra starch in it, for a large
party, was all she ever wore, or wished to
wear; but it was really awful, at Mrs. Brevet-
Major Cobb's time of life—(she dwelt upon
that)—to see her so worldly-minded. As to herself, she hoped her thinking of one little adorn-
ment would be forgiven! She desired to find
a white rose somewhere, just to pin in over
her left ear; nothing so sweetly simple for
a young girl as a rose with a bud—it must
have a bud!—but they were hard to get
good. She had been *twice* to London to

find a rose, and hunted up and down. At last, she was obliged to go to Madame Dudan's. A sweet woman, Madame Dudan! —but, poor thing! in such darkness; however, she made all the court flowers. And, after deliberating, she had ordered the rose from Madame Dudan's, and she had promised her such a bud! The worst feature in poor Mrs. Cobb's case, was the *time* she gave to those vanities. The absolute time!

And so she twittered; never supposin there was a large beam in her own smal eye. Our native fishmonger was offended— he who served the country for five miles around; and yet Mrs. Brevet would get her fish from Billingsgate. The chicken butcher, too—goodness! to think of Mrs. Brevet's saying there was not a turkey fit to eat on the Heath. She who had eaten nothing else for years. And so it went on, from one tradesman to another; then such a furious cabal was got up against the Cobbs by the unasked. One old gentleman appealed to the rector to

arbitrate, as he wished to demand of the
major, why he had not been invited! And
the rector laughingly suggested that the matter should be referred to the bishop. Another
went about declaring that he had as good a
right to be invited as such an 'individual,'
but that it was sometimes more than con-
venient to ask those who looked to be asked
wherever they lent their soup-ladles and
apostle spoons. It was rumoured that a new
carpet had been ordered for the drawing-
room, and that the upholsterer had agreed to
take the old one, as part payment; but that
was clearly proved to be a slander, and was
traced home to somebody — I forget who.
Jerry, next to the dinner-giving lady herself,
enjoyed the turmoil more than any one on the
Heath. To think of Miss Helen upsetting
every one — man, woman, and child, and
caring nothing about it, not a ha'porth. And
Miss Ryland had asked her what she was
going to wear, for surely the poor thing's heart
was fairly tossicated with the enquiry of what

will she wear, what will she wear, and just
wished to be able to tell for satisfaction. And
Miss Helen, the easily pleased craytschur, in
her light-hearted way, had said she certainly
should wear shoes and stockings—and a dress;
and Miss Ryland's own belief was that she had
never given a thought to the dinner, and
charged Miss Ryland not to let her forget the
day. "Oh!" Jerry would conclude, clasping
his hands in an ecstacy—"if Mrs. Brevet Major
Cobb knew that, wouldn't she go stark staring mad! She wonders if Miss Helen doesn't
tell every one—she is going to dine with her
old friends at Hamptead, Major and Mrs. Cobb,
the friends of her childhood—that's the grand
paw! Mrs. Major has invited all 'the dear Horse-
Guard boys' to a ball in the evening, to meet
her sweet *protégé*—the celebrated H.L.—Miss
Helen Lyndsey, born, bred, and reared on the
Heath!"

Mrs. Bruce's soup-ladles, and apostle spoons,
were certainly there, and Mrs. Bruce herself
—a tiny, pale-faced, violet-coloured woman,

who blazed in a clan-tartan and highland bonnet—just as they dress Helen Magregor on
the stage—she went, it was maliciously ru-
mured by some one, to look after her spoons.

Well, the eventful day came at last. Such
savoury smells as came with it from the great
Cobb kitchen, and were wafted over the lawn,
never 'wandered at their own sweet will'
before in the same locality; the poor little
major's dignity was laid aside, and he puffed
up and down the hill with message after message, and almost to the last moment, because
there was nobody else to send. He was seen
to rush towards the fishmonger's, in search of
lobsters, which had not been sent from London
with the turbot. There was one noble
fellow on the board, firm and bright in his
scarlet-coat of shell—a very prince of his kind
—a monarch amongst lobsters—the major
seized upon him.

"Sold, sir," said the fishmonger, emphatically.

"Nonsense!" was the reply; "I don't care
what he costs."

" Sold, sir," repeated the man.

" Double his value ! "

" Sold, sir."

" I must say," exclaimed the irritable major, " that this is not the way to treat an old customer."

" Those as finds turbot, ought to find lobsters," replied the fishmonger, laying the tempting fish upon the tray, and then calling to his boy to take it to Mrs. Dolland.

The major remembered how poor little Mrs. Dolland had been 'snobbed' and cut, and not invited either to dinner or to tea, and felt the case was hopeless ; he could not ask Mrs. Dolland to give up the lobster under the circumstances ; disappointment, and the dread of what Mrs. Cobb would say, overcame his irritation, and turning up his little, fat, humid eyes to the fishmonger, he inquired—" What *am* I to do?—it is a quarter past four now."

" Shrimps, sir !" suggested the fishmonger, turning them carelessly over with his pint measure, " fine shrimps, sir ! I heard of a

lady once who preferred them to lobsters ; but
it ain't general; though a little beet-root
shredded in is a great deception."

"Shall I take shrimps, then ?" mused the
major.

"As you please, sir—shrimps is shrimps,
when they're fresh."

The poor major pocketed the shrimps, and
panted home.

This of course, was but one, amid a host of
petty vexations, which attend an attempt to
get up a gigantic dinner, in a small house,
and with ill trained servants; not all the
money in the world, not all the made dishes
supplied by the most experienced of cooks,
not the finest wines in the oldest cellars, can
make a dinner 'go off' with the quiet and
ease, and perfect routine, which belongs only
to establishments, where dinner giving is part
of the business of the season. I do not of
course, mean that people who do not 'give
dinners,' should not ask their friends to dine,
that indeed, would be paying a tax to display,

at which every honest English heart would revolt; it is the assumption of a magnificence, and expenditure, to which persons have no right, that I think so contemptible, because of its falsehood. If little five hundred a-year, dines with great five thousand a-year in his majestic dining-hall, and sees that five thousand a-year has four men servants in the room, who move about with the precision, but *not* the noise of clock-work, and do everything at the right time, and put everything in the right place, as if by inspiration, why must little five hundred a-year have four hired waiters in his little parlour when great five thousand a year dines with him—waiters who jostle each other—do everything at the wrong time—and put everything in the wrong place? Why will Mrs. Five-hundred-a-year declare she would rather never give a dinner at all, unless she gave it ' properly ?' by which she does not mean a neat, cosy, and well-dressed dinner, such as an English wifely woman arranges in her home-loving

way, particularly when her husband is certain
to be at home, and the welsh leg of mutton,
with its pretty white frill and tiny shape of
currant jelly, is considered the '*piece de resis-
tance,*' which that Frenchman raves about in
his new cookery book, that, by the way, is not
a bit better than poor old Mrs. Glasse, whose
best receipts I copied into 'The young lady's
receipt book,' before I was fourteen years old!
Oh! that all the 'Five-hundred's-a-year,'
would be hospitable in a small, true, kindly
way; not one of those who drink champagne,
or eat imitation dishes, and are jostled by
make-believe footmen, are for a moment disposed to consider them anything but very
silly people, who assume as a fact that visiting
'five-thousand-a-year,' is the same as possess-
ing it.   But I am always restless in this history, wandering away from my subject in a
manner I ought to be ashamed of; after all,
perhaps the most quiet, observant livers are the
most suggestive; for very busy people have
not time to think of what passes around them;

it is like looking into a kaleidoscope, where
nothing is clearly remembered, except the confusion.

The dinner-day and hour arrived. I always
think it unpardonable not to present oneself
at the exact time specified—so the church-
clock struck five as I entered the hall-door,
closely followed by the Misses Saunders. We
found the little major on the hearth-rug,
looking (for him) pale and fatigued, but polite
and kind as ever; and he did not fail
to compliment us on our punctuality;
he introduced us, as was then the custom, to
Captain Wortley and Colonel Ives, ' old brother officers,' and I was glad to see the worthy
major supported by such perfect gentlemen.
Certainly, in all its bearings, either in peace
or war, we may be proud of our soldiers; our
officers *are* soldiers, and our soldiers deserve to
be officers. I ought to forget all those feelings now, I suppose, and think a black coat
most worthy of my admiration; but my heart
throbs at the scarlet; and I never see a blue

jacket, and a little shiny hat—even on the stage—without my eyes becoming more dim than usual, and my feeling a strong desire to be able to do something—no matter what—to show my devotion to the 'army and navy.' It is, I suppose, the same sort of desire which poor Jerry explained by saying—"He only wished Miss Helen, God bless her! was starving, to prove how glad he'd be to beg for her through the world."

Suddenly, Mrs. Cobb flourished in, all smiles and graciousness; and if it had not been for the red and orange turban, and the bird-of-paradise (a double plume, fastened in the centre by a very large carbuncle) she would have been really well dressed; for her gown was of rich black Spanish silk; and, after all, as every one at that time rolled things round their heads *à la Turc*, even the turban was not *outré*, as it would be now.

"I am so disappointed," whispered the youngest Miss Saunders, who sported the white rose *and the bud* where she had proposed to place it—just over the left, very large, flat ear—" I am *so disappointed ;* why, she looks *quite respectable !"*

The company (six-and-twenty were invited to dinner) flocked in : some I knew, some I did not know ; but I was at no loss to discover the most influential, by Mrs. Cobb's manner. One general-officer, his wife, and daughter, occasioned a grander reception than I could describe. It was now half-past five, and Helen had not arrived. Mrs. Cobb's eyes were directed towards the window, which commanded the gate of entrance : suddenly, I saw her features assume a most perplexed expression, and, as suddenly, the dissonance of a whole band of marrow-bones and cleavers broke upon us. Those 'dear Horse-Guard boys' threw up the windows in an ecstasy, and Mrs. Cobb exclaimed, in a voice most earnestly and unaffectedly tragic—

" Oh, Cobb, Cobb ! who has done this ?"

Some *malignant* had certainly sent those disturbers of the public peace and Mrs. Cobb's

triumph, to commence their hideous noise upon
Helen's arrival, for before Mrs. Cobb's sentence was finished, the young lady had
entered, evidently much amused at the din
which greeted her approach; the heightened
colour on her cheeks, and the brightness of her
eyes, seemed produced by the mirthful spirit
that had taken possession of her; while her
slight, little graceful figure, dressed in India
muslin, gave her altogether such a child-like
look, that those who had never seen her before,
seemed as though they could not believe she
was really 'H. L.' She looked as light and
bright as a sun-beam, trying to escape from
Mrs. Cobb's imprisoning arms.

The poor lady was pouring forth all sorts
of apologies—the major had quitted the room
to dismiss the minstrels, who insisted upon
being paid for the hour, during which their
services had been ' bespoke,' as they declared,
by him—not in person—but by message.

Helen, true to her love of mischief, would
persist in thanking her hostess for the compli-

ment thus conveyed; and it was some time
before poor Mrs. Brevet, passing one yellow
arm, bony and strong of muscle, round the fair,
white shoulder, of the blushing, laughing girl,
led her pompously to the different matrons,
and introduced her—first, of course, to the
general's lady.

"I have the honour—the pleasure to
present to you, my highly-gifted young
friend—the poetess, and dramatist—H. L.
—Miss Helen Lyndsey." This was repeated three or four times, until Helen,
finding it impossible to endure it longer,
rushed to the window, as she said, to take a
last look at the 'Wandering Musicians.' Mrs.
Cobb's agonies commenced anew. "How
could she! so refined as she was—so delicate
—endure such an outrage upon science and
sense! It had always," she informed the
company, "been the practice of their house
to be summoned to dinner by music, and she
should certainly make it a point to discover,
and punish, whoever had dared to play the trick

L 2

which had been played that day. Then in a
whisper to the mirthful Helen, she intreated
her not to laugh.   Why should she laugh?
it was cruel, and surely she would not wound
the feelings of the ladies to whom she had not
been introduced, by refusing them the pleasure
they desired 'so earnestly;' and this time
she almost dragged Helen from the window,
who held back like a froward child, half smiling, half pouting, and evidently displeased, at
being made a show of; but Mrs. Brevet
clutched her victim the more firmly, and
by the time the presentations were over, I saw
that Helen was decidedly in an ill temper.
The gentlemen intreated the same favour;
and were marched up to where poor Helen had
fallen into a chair, longing for the announcement of dinner, to save her from greater
suffering.

While a very grave gentleman was performing a well considered and frequently practised
bow, his feet in the first position, Helen,
whose nerves were already over taxed, sprung

from her chair so abruptly, that their
heads came in contact, and the grave elderly
gentleman staggered back. The *gong* had
thundered forth its intimation that the dinner
was served, with such emphasis, that Helen
was not the only lady present whom the sound
electrified. Miss Saunders, white muslin bud
and all! threw herself into the the arms of the
tallest of those 'dear Horse Guard boys,' who
were standing near her, and who held her off
at arms' length, instead of shielding her
timidity in his bosom! In fact, all
the ladies were thrown into consternation;
but immediately after, some 'engaged' musicians struck up ' oh the roast-beef of old England,' and the procession formed, not without
much confusion, however, though the major displayed his military tactics to great perfection,
bringing the human chaos into order in much
less time than I considered possible; this
mêlée agonized poor Mrs. Cobb, who, in
the turmoil, instead of taking the general's
arm, took that of a young cadet, causing in-

finite amusement to the company ; and a more
laughing party never struggled round an
over-crowded dinner table ! Again Helen's
eyes sparkled with mirth and mischief; the
good things of this life had taken the attention
of the company away from her ; and while she
trifled with her fish and soup, she became the
observer, instead of the observed ; she was well
placed between Colonel Ives, and a young
man, who, wonderful to relate, was handsome,
without showing by his manner, that he believed implicitly in the power of his own beauty;
his beauty was however, marred by a certain
sarcastic expression, which particularly, when
his eyes glanced at either the major or
his wife—was anything but pleasant to me.
If hospitality has its duties, it also has its
rights, and surely the giver of the feast, should
be held sacred from ridicule, while ministering
according to his knowledge, to the wishes and
pleasures of his guests. I write this *now*, and
I felt it *then* ; but even in those days of long
and heavy dinners, that dinner was remarkable;

for being overdone in quantity. I have
seldom seen such pyramids of food! there were
not three consecutive inches of table cloth to
be seen in any one spot of the table; wherever a dish of any size could be placed, there it
was sure to be. How a modern dinner-giver
would stare and shudder at such a mixture of
contradictions. The first and second courses
seemed to have been got on, and got off, the
table, by a succession of miracles, the more
surprising, as every body was expected
to help whatever was before him, and
there was a perpetual criss-crossing of
plates, with the explanation—'A slice of that
tongue, if you please'—'A bit of the breast
of the goose, and some stuffing, sir, for a lady'
—'I'm to trouble you, if you please, for some
cauliflower'—and so on. I could see Mrs.
Brevet's head bobbing round, first on one side,
then on the other, really anxious that everybody should eat everything, and calling to her
favourites, at the top of her voice, with the
hope they were 'enjoying their dinner.' Helen

in particular she watched over, as an old
pigeon does over a young one, and would have
crammed her to suffocation if she had been
permitted to do so. The gentlemen all asked
the ladies to take wine; and the master of the
house would have conceived himself wanting
in hospitality, if he had not invited each person
at the table to 'take wine' with him. The
major worked hard, but the fatigues of the
day told upon him, and his marvellous wife
worked 'double tides' in consequence; her
eyes, ears, and tongue neither took nor gave
rest: but then the huge epergne in the centre
prevented her commanding more than one
half the table.

"Major!" she shouted, quite aware of his
deafness, "you are not taking care of your
friends: Miss Lyndsey's wine is in her glass,
and you take no notice." The handsome sarcastic gentleman near Helen whispered something to her, and I saw, by the direction of
his eyes, that it was a severe observation on
Mrs. Cobb: but Helen drew up her head, and

repelled it; I knew she did, by the sheepish
expression which passed over her neighbour's
features, and by the curl on her own lips.

"Abraham and Jones, remove that thing
in the middle," commanded Mrs. Brevet,
"that I may get a full sight of my dinner-
table, and my friends; for the poor major's no
good since he grew so deaf!—a clear field and
no favour," she added: but the removal was
not easily accomplished.

Helen received a blow from an orange, and
Colonel Ives was well peppered with sugar-
plums; the bouquet, which Helen said was
"like a woman, part nature, part art," took
another direction, and was discovered to have
been tied together by — a lady's garter!
This caused a universal titter. Mrs. Cobb
met the difficulty 'like a Briton;' "and sure,"
she exclaimed, "no one need be ashamed of
what kings and queens wear and bestow as a
distinction;" I respected her for that!—if
she had stammered, or explained, or apologized,
they would have improvised an impropriety;

it was excellent. When the confusion subsided
Mrs. Cobb took the command, and the dinner
became exceedingly amusing. The general
and his wife and daughter, and one or two
strangers of high standing, who had been
lured there by the hope of meeting 'H. L.'
looked what they really were—aristocratic and
astonished! but with the ease that always
distinguishes well-bred people, when they recover themselves, they went with the stream,
and were repaid afterwards by the opportunity
of conversing with her whose genius they
earnestly admired; indeed, Helen's full tide
of popularity, surged over all absurdities and
difficulties; the young men believed themselves, one and all, in love with her to distraction : the old, wished to be young again, for
the privilege of falling at her feet, without
being ridiculous. And what pictures those
old gentlemen were !—the spotless white waist-
coats, confined by single buttons over the
exquisite and elaborate shirts; the brilliant
rings and studs, and sleeve-buttons, and knee-

buckles, and shoe-buckles!—the wigs—such
wigs! the stars, and ribbons, and white cam-
bric handkerchiefs—and the ladies vieing with
each other, as to who should have the shortest
waist, and the least quantity of fullness in
their skirts, tucking their dresses so tightly
round them, that it was with difficulty they
got up when once they sat down, freezing even
in the dog-days in a single petticoat—it was
a curious assembly!

. The major's little speech after dinner, pro-
posing Helen's health, ' after the king's,' was
simple and touching; tears, large and heavy
rolled down her cheeks, and yet she owed him
nothing; how difficult it is to trace our emo-
tions to their source. When it concluded, the
major rubbed his little fat hands, and sat
down, while Mrs. Brevet exclaimed, " And is
that *all* you have to say, Brevet Major John
Cobb? Well, I'm sure!"

" I am delighted you thought it well, my
dear," said the little deaf man, who had only
caught that particular word, and he sprang up:

and bowed, "thank-you, my dear. I do enjoy,
ladies and gentlemen, pleasing my wife. We
do not, my married friends, always succeed in
doing so, but when we do—oh!"—and he
smirked, and sat down.

"Heaven help me," she sighed audibly,
"I am so disappointed in the major, he is *so
very deaf!*"

Helen's interesting flirtation with both her
neighbours was broken off at last; she was
again encircled by Mrs. Cobb's loving arm,
and the fairest portion of the gathering
vanished.

The drawing-room was crowded when we
entered, and Helen went through another set
of presentations. Mrs. Cobb was radiant with
triumph; she forgot even the marrow-bones
and cleavers; she *was* the patroness of genius;
she little thought how Helen protected her, turning aside the shafts of ridicule that were aimed
at her, and covering her weakness with the
shield of her own power. Suddenly, however,
she disappeared. I saw the desire to escape,

and covered her retreat, following her down-
stairs; she kissed me in the hall, and insisted
on driving me home, saying I looked ill; and,
indeed, I felt anything but well. .

When the company found she was really
gone, they rapidly followed; all, except those
who scented the hot supper afar off. The
Cobb dinner served as a matter of conversation, to all talkers, for months afterwards; but
there were some present on that occasion,
who never forgot it was *there* they first met
Helen Lyndsey.

CHAPTER VIII.

"We toil through pain and wrong;
   We fight and fly;
We love, we lose, and then, ere long,
   Stone-dead we lie.
O life! is all thy song
   Endure and—die?"

PROCTER.

———

I WAS not much refreshed by sleep, though,
when I awoke, I saw by the beams of light,
which crossed the room, despite the drawn
curtains, that the day was far advanced. I
had the sensation of having been startled, and
not that I had wakened because my sleep was
done; presently, my maid came in—not
creepingly, as if she would avoid disturbing

me, but—as if she desired to rouse me at
once; she looped back the curtains, and the
unbroken flood of light forced me to close my
eyes. She was a jaunty, pretty sort of person,
with a humble, caressing manner, like a
spaniel. I did not quite like her; but she
was very attentive and useful; and, as I gave
her little to do, she seemed well content with
her place—in those days, places were not
called 'situations.' Mrs. Brevet Major said
she was the sixth maid I had—to her knowledge—spoiled—rendered quite unfit for any
other service; and I really think that was
decidedly true. If servants are not perfect in
their business I cannot help it; I cannot
teach; and I told Mrs. Cobb, that following
them would so fatigue me, I preferred
putting up with their neglect to correcting it.
What contempt that strong-bodied, strong-
minded woman must have had for me; I remember thinking so that very morning.

Lucy did not know I was awake; but she
wanted to waken me; she moved my dressing-

chair, and a small library-table, to where I
had left it the night before ; and then I asked
myself the question, by whom had it been removed. I saw her hand straying among my
papers, in an accustomed, friendly sort of
manner; and I observed her press the folding
of a letter, I had received from Helen, down with
her nail, as if she knew exactly how it ought
to be folded. I felt I should not leave
my letters about in that careless manner. I
remembered poor Jerry once thanking God
very earnestly that he had never the luck to
be able to read what he called ' running hand,'
because, if he could have read it, "he was
sure he never could have helped reading every
scrap of writing that came in his way, it was
so mighty tempting to find out so asy what
everybody thought ; and yet, somehow, he
believed it not quite right."

After Lucy had folded the letter, she patted
it into its place, then surveyed the table, and
betook herself to make some new noise,
upon which I sat up, and asked her why she

disturbed me. She told me it was ten o'clock,
and that Mr. Marley was waiting breakfast for
me, in the parlor.

'Waiting breakfast,' that was cool! Why
I had never asked him to breakfast. I did not
hurry, and was as chilling to him, as I could
be to any one in my own house. I had made
up my mind what to say before I entered, to
question him, and induce him to speak of
Helen; 'induce' him! Why, at first he
talked of nothing else! it was nothing but
Helen, a very little about Florence, 'but
Helen!'

It was quite impossible to withstand the fascination of his manners, to avoid listening, and
being pleased when he wished to please; he
gave no time for question, or remonstrance, he
desired to make no impression that was faint or
imperfect, he seemed as anxious to conciliate
me, as he had once been indifferent to my
opinion. He lamented the evil tongues of the
world which had given him a wrong idea of
Helen—Helen, whom he had known all her

life. Helen's father had been almost his
guardian. I asked if he had known Helen's
mother, the question seemed to spring naturally
from his observation, yet it was one of my
unfortunate hits; his colour changed, his lips
became white and trembling, and something
very like a curse escaped them. He could
not or would not answer me, but rose from the
table and turned to the window. I imputed
his agitation to resentment against the woman
who had abandoned her husband in the hour of
his greatest need, and stumbled out a few
remarks as to woman's duty, adding, that
such a woman as Mrs. Lyndsey, never could
be expected to act as Florence, for instance,
under similar circumstances would have acted;
this led him to speak of Florence, could I
wonder at his desire to hasten his union
with Florence—would I use my influence
with her father to accelerate it—only, he
must entreat me not to mention the subject
before Helen. Helen whom he had always
regarded as a child, but much to his per-

plexity (he was not a vain man), but it was
unfortunately made evident to him, that
Helen had imagined the care and interest he
bestowed upon her and her father, arose from
a more tender feeling than friendship could
inspire ; he enlarged upon this with a frank-
ness and yet a delicacy that I was ashamed
not to appreciate more highly.   I felt sure that
in some way or other he was deceiving me, and
yet, such was his power, I was angry with
myself for the suspicion.   He added, that
while he regretted this, he felt assured such
was the volatility of Helen's nature, that
when he was united to Florence or even
before then, her fancy would find some other
object ; he did not for a moment, *now*—oh not
for an instant believe the whispers against
Helen, which seemed to come from the four
winds, so impossible was it to trace them ;
but it was a source of the greatest anxiety to
him, as her friend, who had done his best to
shield her from her own imprudence ; he felt
bound to protect her, and yet his protection
brought her trouble.

I said I had known her from her earliest childhood, but had never heard of him.

"Truly! but when she went abroad, what was she but a child?"

Now this conversation, so dulcet, so reasoning, so suggestive, to what did it lead? to render me suspicious, more than ever suspicious of the marvellous creature whose genius he extolled, whose *morale* he depreciated; yet I could lay hold of nothing. I told him I would question Helen, for I was certain she did not feel the smallest particle of love for him, and I would prove it; and without wounding my *amour propre*, he gave me to understand that I could not cope with her, that she could make me believe just what she pleased, and had boasted of it; that of course she would deny the preference if I were to allude to it; it was painful; he hoped I would not misunderstand his motive, he had the most exalted admiration of Helen, but he knew her violent and passionate nature, and her intense hatred of Florence. He knew she would go any lengths to prevent their union. Such was Helen's pride of power, that as she would stop at nothing, he hoped I would see the necessity for preventing all intercourse between the cousins; it was a knowledge of her jealous nature, coupled with a story which he now considered utterly false, that had once driven him beside himself, and, he feared, made him forgetful of the respect he owed to the beloved friend of his beloved Florence.

I told him that if Helen were jealous of him, as he said, on the one hand, Florence had apparently good cause for the same feeling, on the other. He was in constant attendance upon Helen. Nothing could be more marked than his conduct at the theatre. If he wished to cure her of a hopeless passion, that was not the way to do it.

Marley shook his head, and gave sound to those detached sentences which, according to the ordinary reading, imply a great deal or nothing —assured me "I little knew"—that "hereafter

he might feel justified in being more explicit"
—that her father's condition cast her upon
him—that, with all his admiration, he would
not attempt to conceal from my penetration
(my 'penetration,' Heaven help me!) that
Helen Lyndsey's great fault was her want of
truth. "She has never had," he said, "the
slightest value for truth; she has no consciousness of the disgrace of falsehood." Adding with peculiar emphasis—"You *must* know
this."

Alas! what could I say? I knew it but too
well. She never comprehended the sacredness
of truth. It is a grievous confession to make
of one I loved so tenderly. From her earliest
childhood, she attached no possible disgrace
to an untruth. She considered it simply a
ruse of the imagination, and that if a fiction might be written, a fiction might be
told. She did not seem to have the
power to perceive the difference. I could
not contradict Marley in this matter; having
gained that one point, it was astonishing

how he worked it, keeping it before me,
even in all his eulogies—the canker in the
rose, the maggot in the nut; having pained
and bewildered me to that degree, that my
brain whirled, my hands trembled, and, in my
fruitless endeavour at self-possession, I suffered
the urn to flood the tray, and emptied the
sugar-basin into the tea-pot. I was over-
powered by a weight of doubt and misery,
while his full soft voice, like an imperceptible
poison, was surely instilling all evil influences
and suspicions into my mind. I longed to
start up, and, by a strong and sudden effort
to cast off the weight which pressed upon me;
the very atmosphere seemed to enchain me;
the command, "Get thee behind me, Satan,"
echoed in my ears; but the simple fact is, I
am a coward; I think brave thoughts, but
seldom put them into action. I had no faith in
Marley; and yet, such was his skill and tact,
that I was spell-bound; every second minute
he gave utterance to a sentiment, which, at
the instant, made me hate myself for doubting

him; when gradually, and with such tenderness and delicacy he dwelt upon his adoration
of 'the peerless Florence,' my heart opened
at his words; he touched upon the exquisite
and femine qualities of her mind with so much
fervour, that they became more bright in the
light he shed upon them. He sketched the
perfect woman, dreading the public gaze and
shrinking at the world's applause, until, at
least for a little while, I forgot *why* Helen
toiled and worked her golden mine in darkness, until the day of notoriety burst upon it:
he drew no comparison between them, but I
saw clearly what he intended. Well, the frigid
breakfast, and the interview at last came to
a close, and he left me, certainly with the
impression that the less the cousins saw of
each other the better.

Now does this not seem weak and foolish?
that the sophistry of a man, whom I knew in
my heart of hearts, to be unworthy of belief;
in whom I put no trust, and felt no confidence
—should uproot for a time, the desire—should

overthrow the hope of the latter years of my life. I knew the influence was evil, even while I yielded to it. I am often disposed to lay the flattering unction to my soul, that I was worn out, and in weak health; but I know it was more to be attributed to that mental want of firmness, which has so often marred my best resolves. I was then averse to believe what I firmly believe now, that there is some analogy between the mental and bodily conformation of woman, and a poor weak creature, as I always was, without having an imbecile understanding, would be likely to indulge that softness of heart, and pliancy of temper, which create an indolent and inactive character. I know my want of strength, and from that knowledge, has arisen a habit, to which I have been deeply indebted, when sorely perplexed by contending feelings, or when I have not known what to choose, when distinct 'facts' have been placed before me. I *think* a prayer; were it thrown into words, it would be held too simple and childish, to be of any value. Sometimes a line, or it may be two, of the hymns I learned leaning beside my mothers knee, pass through my memory, and as it were direct and sanctify my judgment. I do not know how it, is, I only know that after such a petition, I have always been guided right. Fortunately for me, I was taught to consider prayer, as a prescription, which should stand analysis and examination. And those little prayer texts, which my mother set up as finger posts for my spirtual life, were indications of the grandest, and holiest truths; they came at my bidding, freighted with comfort and wisdom. But it is a positive fact, that in Marley's presence, I *could not* exercise this thought-prayer, which at all times else would come as soon as my pleading spirit sought it. These prayer-thoughts always resembled the sun, giving light before they gave heat; but when he spoke, when his presence, his atmos- phere, filled the room, I was as his slave!

I believe Marley thought he had quite won me to think his thoughts. He endeavoured to extract a promise that I would use my influence, and every other means, to keep the cousins apart; but I resolutely refused to give any promise, or to be bound to any line of conduct; I had strength left for that, which truly was not much, and when his dangerous influence was removed and after calm consideration, and prayer, which returned when he departed with more than ordinary fervour, I could not but feel how poor and pitiful I was, how unworthy to be called by the holy name or friend, how unfitted for the prompt action which commands respect! Surely I had dreamed away more than half my life, and instead of feeling ashamed of such dreaminess, I had been secretly content to consider that I fulfilled all womanly duties, because I was calm and quiet, and avoided with more carefulness of self than became a Christian woman, all troublesome straits and difficulties; I had given myself credit for being meek and patient, when I should have been brave and outspoken

I referred to the past, and though I had done
what at the time I thought 'my best,' I now
felt that if I had been as faithful as affectionate,
during Helen's childhood, she might have been
different from what she was.   Then self-
gratulation whispered—" You did your best,"
while conscience, sturdy with me for once,
said, "You did not." I know, as I know
now, that public voice, public fame, however
it may agitate, can never fill a woman's
heart. I knew that a woman in the full
blaze of public life, can never enjoy the
sanctity that, combining with the privacy of
home, makes it an earthly heaven; but my
poor Helen had no home.   What is home, but
the sweet circle of loving relatives—precious
friends—and duties it is a privilege not a task
to perform! was she to be for ever shut out
from such enjoyments, or was she altogether
formed for another destiny? what should I
do—how manage—must I dissimulate, or
should I boldly tell the truth? what 'truth'
had I to tell?   What fact to build upon? did

I believe in Helen as in a true thing? alas! no, in Marley? *no, no!* And Florence, should I arise and be doing? doing what? faithfully—faithfully, and right were they who named me 'NOBODY.'. I observed and compared, but how little did I *do*! surely there were women—hard handed, hard working women in the nooks and corners of the world, in alleys, and courts, and hospitals—in garrets, and areas—in rooms, where pure daylight never entered, who *had called themselves* into an activity, and done deeds of love and charity —benevolence, and earnest work, that should put a race of such do-nothings as myself to shame and confusion. I was ever desirous of doing something, and ended by doing nothing. Half the day was gone, yet I sat there still, winking in the sunbeams, whenever I raised my aching eyes, and waiting rather for the progress of the earth, than rousing myself to draw the curtain! Alas! alas! how we dream through life, and how anxious are the dreamers to cast the reproach

of restlessness and unquiet—on the workers.
Oh, for a crucible to convert musing into
thinking, and intention into action.

By a violent effort I remember gathering
home my thoughts so as to attend to the
letters that heaped my table.—The general
small change of correspondence contains nothing, so there are nothing to write about ; and
that moulding a phrase, and turning a sentence so as to give the most graceful substance to nothing, is a matter of difficulty.   I
got through my task, however, and sent Jerry
with the letters to the post-office.   Poor Jerry
disliked letters ; he always said no good came
of them, that it was far better for people to wait
till they met, and thus have out whatever they
had to say ; he associated a letter with a challenge, and thought every note a ' message,'—
according to the then reading of the word.   I
remember his entering—while balancing himself, as usual, on one leg—into a long detail
of how ten of the finest gentlemen in his
county all got shot out of one ' letther !'

It began—the misunderstanding—by a gentleman, talking of foreign parts, saying, he
had seen anchovies growing upon trees; and
some one said, he would not have the heart to
write such a lie; and he said, he would not
only write it, but send it in a letter, which, of
course, was a challenge. Well, two fought
about that, and the person who made the
assertion, just before he died explained that he
did not mean anchovies—he meant barnacles.
And Jerry added, "there seemed as much
sense in the one as in the other." But the
seconds took up the dispute, and fought there
and then, and one was *kilt*, and the other
killed ; and then, according to Jerry (who had
more than a common delight in talking of
duels, or, as he called them 'jewels,' though
he pretended to be shocked at them), the
friends of the principals and seconds took up
the quarrel, one with another, and there
seemed no end of the fearful loss of life which
followed this absurdity.. "And all along of a
letther, ma'am dear, that's the worst of it—

nothin' but a letther; no wonder I've no heart
to them for letthers! But, ma'am, I don't
think I've made myself intelligent to ye, or,
maybe again, it's not well you are! Ah, if
yer honour was on the top of the mountain
that hangs over my people—the green valley,
with the bright river running through it, just
as the spirit puts life into the body—and the
birds! Ah, then! never—never, nowhere, in
no part of the world, have I ever heard music
to equal the song of the thrush, of a summer
morning, out of the old grey thorn, that
flourished like a ruin just by the bed of that
singing river! Oh, I wish to my heart you
were alone, on that mountain, and it's
a strong, brave, hearty lady you'd be then;
there's no air here fit for a mortial to breathe;
no air—nothing to give strength! and sure its
ashamed of meeself I ought to be for bothering
you: so I'll take the letter, ma'am, and God
bless you, and make the heavens above yer
bed, when ye'r tired of this mortial life."

I ought to have gone to Helen. I ought,

to have gone to Florence. I desired, yet
dreaded, to see Mr. Middleton. Marley had
confused and embittered all my thoughts
and feelings. I ought to have ordered the
carriage. I rose up, ordered it, went to my
room to change my dress, but instead of doing
what I ought to do, and desired to do, I did
what I could not avoid; I went to bed.

178

CHAPTER IX.

"Dreams we would make realities; life seems
So changed in after time,
That we would wish realities were dreams."

SWAIN.

LONG before day-break, I was so ill with a
trotting pulse, and a beating brain, that my
maid (for whom I had hardly power to call)
sent for my doctor, who was the doctor of the
district. Even then, doctors were more important, and of greater importance than they
are now; all the Heath held Dr. Brough in awe;
children would move reverently out of his way,
while his eye was on them, and then set off at

full gallop as if 'Bogie' were at their heels.
Every body knew the sound of his horse's
hoofs, and many peeped over their blinds,
or drew back their curtains, stealthily to
see him pass. He was, like nearly all his
profession, lavish in kindness—the practical
working of every division of charity was in his
hand, giving to those who needed both money
and medicine, watching, ay, and praying too,
where no one else would watch or pray,
instant in and out of season, and yet rough,
and blunt at times, so that the wealthy sick
rejoiced when he was gone; while the poor
regretted they got well so soon. When once
he paid a visit, he was certain to be retained;
for who would change if they could help it,
a father-confessor, a doctor, or a dentist?
My doctor was somewhat above the middle
height, and carried his head erect, as if he
honoured it, as the noblest part; his step
was firm and deliberate, and yet soft, it never
alarmed any body—his eyes, grey and restless,
were observant rather from habit, than from

curiosity or shrewdness—his voice was tuneless,
even when his words were tender or hopeful,
indeed ' tender' they seldom were, except to
children—his visits were short—his questions
shorter, put somewhat abruptly—he waited
patiently for answers ; but if you attempted to
enlarge, or give him information he did not
require, he would gather his overhanging eye-
brows into a ridge, and say, " be so good as
to confine your answers to my questions ;"
perhaps he would then pause, consider, and
ask another. If there were twenty books upon
the table, he would look at the title page of
each, and there was a play of expression about
his mouth, which at once told those who knew
him the opinion he entertained respecting
them. He was a wonderful reader, though he
never seemed to take pleasure in what he
read. Whenever he requested a lady to
put out her tongue, he usually begged her
pardon, and apologized for being under the
disagreeable necessity of ordering medicine,
instead of confections. He was always re-

markably well dressed, (not as physicians
dress now). Dr. Brough would have considered
it an insult if a brother practitioner met him
in consultation in a frock coat, or trowsers.
He was himself got up to admiration in silk
stockings, diamond knee buckles, a peculiarly
square cut coat, the snowy frill of his shirt
delicately pleated and folded down under a
most elaborate waistcoat; but his cravat, so
many and so massive were its folds, that his
thin narrow, yellow face, looked as if escaping
from a turban. If nature had not given him
a very long neck, he must have been suffocated : that cravat was a standing miracle to
me. I can see it now; whenever I hear
the word 'exaggerated,' poor Dr. Brough's
cravat unrols before my eyes. I was never
so ill, that I did not long. to ascertain
how many yards of muslin were employed in
its construction, but thought it would be mean
and unbecoming to ask his housekeeper. Al·
though the doctor's face was yellow, and his
nose a *little* crimsoned at the end, yet his

hands were well formed, and white as snow,
and his ring perfection : a coolness sprang up,
which lasted several years, between Miss
Saunders and Mrs. Brevet Major, about that
ring; Miss Saunders stoutly asserting that it
was a *real* diamond, which Mrs. Cobb contra-
dicted by declaring (accompanied by a con-
temptuous observation on Miss Saunders's
want of judgment) that it was only paste !
The doctor could have decided the matter, but
who would have ventnred to ask him ?   Certainly, he afforded his patients, friends, and
acquaintances sufficient opportunities of judging of the ring; for it was everywhere, wandering like some particular star, amid the
mazes of his well-curled Brutus (wig), on the
table, sparkling here, reposing there, folding
and unfolding his snowy handkerchief, or resting, in dignified placidity, upon his knee.

When on horseback, he always paused at
his own door to survey the poorer class of
patients, who awaited his going and coming:
and I must repeat that to the poor the good

doctor was an unchanging friend; he would leave his comfortable bed on the bleakest night that ever December snowed upon earth, to attend a poor neighbour, though perfectly convinced he could never receive a farthing for his attendance; but no matter who waited, he always paused at his own door, drew off his glove, and patted his horse's neck in the most patronizing manner; this movement exhibited the ring to great advantage, and once on a time, Jerry, quite unconsciously, travestied the beggar woman's compliment to the beautiful Duchess of Devonshire; for, with one of his most obsequious bows, he asked the doctor, "if his honour would let him light his pipe at his ring." Poor dear Dr. Brough, *after* that, declared the Irish were the best-bred and most intelligent people in the world! and Jerry was seldom passed without a smile and a sixpence.

I really do not know what the good doctor said was the matter with me; I was just in that nervous state of half suffering, half shame, that I did not care what became of me.

I felt so powerless, so bewildered, that I
despaired, in the bitterness of my trembling
spirit, of being acceptable in the sight of
God, because of my lack of usefulness, either
in my own or others' vineyards. This more
than usual trial of despondency was accompanied with bodily prostration, and I felt
as if I was not worth the expense of
the doctor's prescription. He flourished his
handkerchief, and displayed his ring, and
I could have quarrelled with his usual
absurdity of begging my pardon combined
with the command of "put out your tongue,"
but I was glad to do what I was desired as
quickly as possible.   "Oh!" he said, as if reading my thoughts, "I remember all about Helen
Lyndsey, when she wrote verses, and you cor-
rected them! your brain has been overworked,
my dear madam! I said to Major Cobb last
night, the wit and the imagination belong to
'H. L,' but the observation, the development
of character, come from our neighbour. Nay,
I shall not hear one word of denial, or explana-

tion, not one word! my dear lady I know it!
the major differed from me, he was superficial
enough to say, that he never heard *you* talk
in blank verse! and then the next moment he
confessed he had heard you utter the same
opinions in prose; not one word! you must
excuse me, I am too much a man of the world
not to know that a lady's denial is almost an
admission. Oh, it is quite evident—feverish
pulse—hot hand—burning brow! Your mind
is too active, you are too energetic.

I endeavoured to get in a word.

"Yes, I know you will deny it; the most pro-
found thinkers affect all that, they cloak themselves in silence, and prefer concentration to
display. It is unfair, though, I must say, that
your pupil should have all the honour, while
you!—now, why attempt to deny it? nothing
but the excitement of a first representation
could account for these symptoms. Yes, yes,
I know; but, really, you shall not talk—
you must keep quiet. Oh! very well; if you
command of course I shall obey, and deny the
fact."

Doctor Brough's laugh was detestable—it was a barking sort of convulsion—short and abrupt; and, gentlemanly as he was, he looked hideous when he laughed. I became really angry, and denied, as well I might, participation in the authorship. He bowed; and, in a quiet, calm way, which was a hundred times more provoking than his former accusations, he said that, of course, every one had a right to the possession of their own secret, only that he imagined to an old friend I might have been more candid. He only regretted that what he had said added to the excitement, from which already I suffered so much that I should never hear a word from him again on the subject, delighted as he had been with the play, such a house crowded to the ceiling, and the play announced as 'H. L.'s' by the manager.

"Now I must keep calm, I really must— quite cool, and calm, and not attempt to move or think."

And so he bowed himself out, and left me,

more anxious—more worried—more miserable
and undecided than I was when he came.

I heard afterwards that, the same evening,
when Florence Middleton quitted the dining-
room and entered the ante-room I have already
mentioned, she was startled by seeing the
round, grizzled head of Jerry projected between the window-curtains.

"Whisht, Miss Florence, darling—whisht!
don't mind, dear—sure it's only Jerry; and
I've had the thieving of the world to get here,
I have—I mean thieving my way up to the
house ; if I tould any of the servants I wanted
ye, it's for blaring out they'd be, at the top of
their voice ; and I want you to come out to
the heath, Miss, *on the sly*, to give them the
slip, dear, for it's a thousand contrivances there
is to keep you from those you ought to be with.
Well, never mind ; maybe I'm wrong ; and, if
I am, why I am ; but the poor mistress is ill,
agra !—mighty sick, and only mistress Lucy
with her—and she's no great shakes, that's
one thing—and no comfort, and that's another

—so come, dear Miss Florence, and lave a bit of a note for your papa, just to insense him into it; and come, if you plaze, Miss, to lave the note in your papa's room; and will I bring a carriage—will I, miss, at once?"

While Jerry went for the hackney coach, which he would have conceived it an insult to name to Florence as other than 'a carriage,' Florence sought Mrs. Dellamere in her dressing-room, just as the knitting-needles had fallen from her soft fingers, and she was dozing off into a gentle slumber, and told her their dear NOBODY was ill. Mrs. Dellamere had a decided belief that every ailment was, or would be, fever; and so she bustled back to the dining-room, and trumpeted my situation to the gentlemen, of whom Marley was one. He, with his usual blandness, suggested that he knew of my illness; but, as he did *not* know *what turn it might take,* had not mentioned it before Florence, whose tender love for me would at once have urged her to my bedside; "and, dear Mrs. Dellamere," he

added, " who can tell the consequences ? " The
result was, that Florence was intercepted in
the hall, and had to endure the anticipations
of all evil from Mrs. Dellamere, while Marley
and her father entreated her to wait, at all
events, until morning.

The hall door was open, and there stood
Jerry at the coach door ; he could not, of
course, resist interfering.

" If it's plasing to you, Mr. Middleton, sir,
do ye think the mistress would send me for
Miss Florence, if she had any bad sickness
about her ? "

Marley turned upon him, and coolly asked
if he had been sent.

" Sent !—listen to that now ! Is it the
bouldness I'd have to come, barring I was
sent ? It's long until Miss Florence would put
even such a question as that to me ! Sent—
what will I say, Mr. Middleton ?—an' sure it
would be a woeful thing if any badness came
to the poor mistress, that has no one of her
own flesh an' blood to see after her ; and she

mother and gran'mother, and all kind of relations to everybody : 'deed, the doctor as good as said he didn't ' expect her *_____' "

At this point of Jerry's exaggerating eloquence, his ear, which was as quick as his eye, caught a muttered expression of Marley—

" Confound the Irish idiot."

Perhaps Jerry would have passed over the insult to himself, but ' *Irish* idiot ' was a reflection on his country. When speaking of this passage in his life, afterwards, Jerry said—

" I fixed meeself straight in mee shoes— put mee hands behind mee back, to strengthen meeself, and walked up to the slandherer— ' By ye'r lave, sir,' I says, ' I'm not lookin' to do you any damage—only, I just want to whisper a word in your ear.' ' Spake out,' he says, as bould as a ram. ' I will, if it's plasing to you,' I says, ' after I've spoken asy.' The one word did it ; he sprang and shivered as if he'd been shot through the heart, but

---

* ' Expect her '—feared she would die.

steadied himself the next minute as straight as a dart. 'Very good, Jerry,' he says; 'and if it is so, Miss Middleton might go.' Talk of the play actors! Sorra a one at the playhouse ever did the fine innocent gintleman better than that same Mr. Marley. I looked to the very back of his eyes, and they war as clear as a *kitling's*,* and he looked at me again. To be sure, there was a dale of the quality by, and he had nothing else for it; but I wonder how he'd ha' felt on the top of the heath wid me, face to face, and foot to foot, and I talking to him about Miss Helen!"

Mr. Middleton, however, had taken alarm at fever, and would not permit Florence to go until he had seen and questioned the physician. I have forgotten whether it was through Jerry's agency or not, but the next morning it was Helen who was at my bed-side.

I learned so much afterwards, but, for some days, I was almost unconscious of what passed around me — living altogether with

* Kitten's.

the past. My spirit seemed to come and
go; I believed that I—in the spirit—
stood beside the pallid, worn-out frame, in
which I had endured so long. Strange! but
the long past was with me more vividly than
the present; it came, not like forked lightning,
but as if pictured on the mild sheet lightning,
which floods the summer night with silent
brightness—dissolving, to be reproduced—
fresh pictures on the same air-drawn substance, yet how different! My blessed, happy,
fragrant childhood, crowded with loving creatures, to whom I was the promise of much future
happiness—the very memory of that childhood, now, even while I write, thrills me
with joy—that I should, ever so long ago, have
been the centre, the heart, the core of such
a universe of love! Me! a little simple child!
But this fancy faded, and became confused, and the shy, joyous, blushing girlhood
advanced, on tip-toe, like the morning—
buoyant and palpitating on the threshold of
that *love*, which is ever either a woman's bane

or blessing! Calm, and tame, and slow, obr
servant and reserved as I am now, I still say
there is no medium—love is one of the two
—there is no compromising its solemn earnestness—it is 'till death, as regards all that this
world contains of happiness or misery, a
woman's bane or blessing! If my childhood was
supreme in blessings, my girlhood flashed upon
the world, so sunny bright, so full in wealth of
youth, and health, and joy, and riches, that on
I floated, radiant with happiness, and never
doubting its endurance; and then, within one
little week, the heavens changed, there was no
more blue sky—no more bright sunshine; the
atmosphere became heavy, and dark, and
suffocating; my youth dropped from around
me, as it had been a garment, and left nought
but withered flesh and dry bones. My young,
undisciplined, and passionate heart was crushed;
and my hair blanched by the sufferings of a
single day, which seemed like an eternity.
My youth was gone; I doubted if it had ever
been. Death, failure, and falsehood had made

my life a ruin. I struggled from amid the
chaos—the wreck of my young self—each
hope I cherished totally destroyed. I loathed
all memories—I fled from them, as travellers
flee from the sirocco. I turned, with the rapidity of thought, and sprang over them with
one mad leap back to my childhood, and
nestled there in safety and in love. This was
all that HAD BEEN, of which my then world—
any more than my present—knew nothing;
and in that sickness my spirit passed through
it again, save that the darker passages were
softened into sadness—a sadness without sorrow; they had worked me good. Then, after
a little, my spirit called my childhood back
with such reality, that I could press myself
into the faith that I had passed through *two*
childhoods, living over the first in the second,
joy by joy, again and again—waking or sleeping, I lived within this childhood. I cannot
explain what is unexplained to myself. There
were times during that illness I felt myself a
disembodied child, whispering delights to the

aged woman to whom I belonged, and who belonged to me.

As I do live to write this record, I *heard* rustlings of angels wings; and, although I saw them not, I *felt* their presence; were it not dangerous so to think, I could believe they whispered to me; no messages from souls sealed up in silence by the eternal law, but repetitions of those sweet hymns my mother's soft and melting voice poured on my heart like incense; and those deep, thrilling texts that lift us up to heaven! I do believe that illness saved my life, I have learned silence in so stern a school, that my feelings—all too strong, even now, for this poor frame—shake the foundation, giving no outward sign. I was torn and bewildered by conflicting circumstances. Had I been well, Helen had decided I should be her chaperone, and the duty would certainly have killed me—night after night, the heat and crowd, the dazzling triumph of one hour blasted by the detraction and foul envyings of the next! I recovered slowly, and then poor Helen poured out her heart's great secret. She loved! She had loved long and hopelessly, and had but just learned that her passion was returned. The object of this affection was a man, of course according to Helen, the like of whom the world could produce but once in a century; but he had conventional ideas of woman, a sort of eastern theory, that would enfold her in gauze, surround her with perfumes, and feed her on rose confections. His mother, Helen said, crossed their course of love because she could learn nothing of Helen's mother. She believed in hereditary propriety; and would never consent to receive as a daughter one whose mother was not as rigid as herself. Helen appealed to me, as knowing that her mother's fame was *sans tâche,* and, for the first time, seemed to derive pleasure from the remembrance of how that mother scorned and scouted every woman who was not a very dragon of virtue. She remembered a famous denunciation she was fond of uttering against the 'Foundling Hospital,' and against all who harboured boy or girl that came thence into their service; if either, in their infancy, had sheltered under the protection of its extensive roof, she was indignant that the children of 'such creatures' should be taught to sing the praises of God in tune. Strangely as I thought it, Helen Lyndsey was practising the chemistry of extracting sweets from bitters; all the hard, uncharitable sayings and doings of her mother towards every unprotected female she had ever met or heard of, her tenacious memory seemed to have treasured up, and now arrayed as so many witnesses in favour of her mother's purity! I was glad she could extract any pleasant memories from such a childhood, and smiled and nodded an acquiescence in her theories, which I should have found it difficult to express.

She complained that, while dowagers, who had been out of fashion, sought to re-establish their influence, and fill their rooms, by securing her as the attraction; and those who, however covered with gauze and gold, found it impossible to ' draw ' anything like fashionable society into their tasteless but expensive *salons*, without her influence ; while, in fact, ' all London '—the fashionable, the artistic, the literary, the overpoweringly rich and vulgar, the dignified poor and proud, even the stately aristocracy—were all at her feet; while her pictures and busts were ' prepared ' for the Royal Academy—her verses sung in the streets (true test of popularity)—her hands modelled—her really plain nose called ' expressive '—her wit feared and wondered at— perfumes, called ' H. L.'s bouquet,' and bonnets advertised as under her patronage,—her cousin had left London to avoid her !

I did not say so, but the want of Florence by the side of my couch—the soothing of her voice, the heaven of her eyes, the inexpressible tenderness, the lovingness of her nature—was a *want* to me, under the influence of which I felt as if half my life had been taken from me.

CHAPTER X.

" ———Each day secures him more,
    His tempters."

                        BYRON.

———

' THE season ' at that time was not prolonged
as it is now, and it had nearly reached to a
close, before I was able to yield to Helen's
solicitations, and accompany her once or twice
into the glittering throng, which bowed at the
new shrine; the most fashionable *réunions*
were over, but she strongly tempted me, by
naming the persons I hoped and wished to
see, whose names were rightly honoured.
Her play still kept undivided possession of the
stage, and she had driven the manager half

frantic by laughing at his entreaties, that
instead of squandering her time, she would
prepare another.   I should not have wondered if the homage she received (which was,
in fact, one of the insanities that seldom
bewilder London for more than one 'season')
had unsettled her mind so completely, that she
was unable to think or work, to do anything,
in fact, but triumph in her popularity; yet
her analyzing powers, her habit of diving and
sifting, her painfully clear mental sight—which
unless accompanied by a large amount of pure
Christian charity, renders a woman both un-
amiable and unhappy—altogether prevented
her enjoying what might have been enjoyed
with innocence and happiness by one not so
well read in much of the hollowness and bitterness of that which settled around her.   I
felt she was only blind on one subject, but as
Mr. Harrington had been obliged to leave
town on some mission connected with that most
mysterious foreign office, where every feature
even in a one year old clerk seems turned into

stone, and all eloquence subsides into doleful silence or bewildering inuendo,—I had no opportunity, as yet, of judging for myself. His mother was a confirmed invalid, whom Helen never saw, though she sent daily to inquire how the Lady Harrington was, and the message was frequently accompanied by a nosegay of exotics, or a basket of fruit; the answer might have been stereotyped:—" Her ladyship's compliments, and she was as usual." I thought this sort of thing very stiff and heartless; but Helen had determined it to be a kindness, and, as heretofore, what she had determined I had not the courage to dispute. Helen had prevailed on me to remain with her for a time to change the air. " You shall not visit my poor skeleton," she said; " it is an old, true saying, that there *is* one in every house; sometimes it is a fact, as mine is, sometimes a tradition." Her features were always agitated when she spoke of her father, and yet she said no presence had ever yielded her the same relief as Jerry's. No matter how much her sleep had been disturbed by her father's

restlessness during the night—and often I
heard him scream and jabber—she came to me
in the morning for a 'look and a kiss,' arrayed
in a simple, graceful toilet, eager to go to her
desk, compose, answer letters, and arrange business, as if she had passed a tranquil night.
She still sat on her little, straight-backed high
chair, and her small hand and tiny wrist
looked like a child's; sometimes, despite her
exertions to conceal it, she was over-wrought,
and then I could observe the blue, hard lines
of the swollen veins in her full, round temples,
and see her pulses throb through the transparent tissue of that little wrist.   Confide in
me as she would, even as she had done, there
was always something left untold, fluttering on
her lips; she either feared me or herself; her old
habit of exaggeration increased by the food it
fed on; the romancing she indulged in might
have been printed; but what most astonished
me was her knowledge of, and ease in, society.
You might have believed her reading was
limited to the 'Court Guide' and the 'Peerage.'

'My lord' or 'my lady' excited her no more than—not as much as—her old acquaintance Mrs. Brevet-Major Cobb; and when, to my mind, a very rude lady of title—though not of birth—told her, after a prolonged stare, that 'she was much disappointed in her, she was just like any other lady,' Helen put on such a penitent, innocent look, and said—" She was very sorry, would she kindly teach her how to look differently." She was so bending, and yet so self-possessed and dignified.

Her knowledge was quite intuitive; one quick, rapid glance of those clear grey eyes, seemed to take in all beneath their dark fringes; and she knew so well what would please—the form, or no form—the bringing down or drawing up her own mind to the minds of others—the starting a fresh idea, flinging down a jewel, and leaving it there, careless who appropriated it! She knew so perfectly when to speak, and when to remain silent; the proper moment to pay a compliment, and the right way in which to receive one; no matter how often she had heard it

before, she appropriated it with a slight inclination of her beautiful head, and that bewitching smile, whose real meaning often
bewildered me. Her nature was sympathetic
—that was one of her great charms; she could
not help feeling with, and for, every sorrow, and
rejoicing in joy as birds at a sunbeam! Light,
and trifling, and fantastic, provokingly absurd
at one moment, and the next grave, acute, and
reasoning; then off again in an ecstacy with
the Parisian bonnet, that graced an empty head,
and dropping suddenly down to an invalid's
rice-guel, or the dangers of potatoe-arrowroot.
She knew, also, the high place which a good
listener always occupies in society, and the
value of the moderate use of eccentricity in a
public character!

'A public character!'—was that really her
destiny? She never sought to shine, and
though she talked well, she could give place
gracefully to others, though she did not like
to be put aside; indeed, all but two or three
of her acquaintances, who had been unsuccess-

ful in literature, and ventured to try a lance with the bright wonder of the time, rather sought to draw her out than to repel her. She never lit her own lamp; her brightness was involuntary. She received her admirers without affectation, and had more patience with the whole tribe of album-bearers, and autograph collectors, and talkers of, and doers of, nothing, than I should have had: it always puts me into a fidget to see a red and gold, or green and gold, volume peep from beneath the folds of a shawl; and though, goodness knows, an autograph is not much to ask, and seems such a simple and easy way of giving pleasure, yet the 'run' upon my young friend for autographs was so immense, that I have known her write in fifteen albums in a morning, and dispatch twenty autographs by post. And all this to the destruction of the *time* that was her gold. There is no greater relief in the world to literary labour than the face of a friend, or the conversation which rests rather than

fatigues the mind; thus the strongest friend-
ships have subsisted between people of the
highest genius, and others of moderate intellect, but warm hearts; there is no such
blessing to an overwrought brain as resting on
a calm, rational friend ; feeling that it is
called on for no exertion, but reposing on the
strength and affection of a plain, honest heart;
whilst, on the other hand, there is nothing that
so thoroughly worries and beats down a pre-
occupied mind as being constrained by the
ways of the world, to listen to, or seem to enter
into, the inane nothings, which are talked
about, and repeated, and turned over and
over to no purpose by men and women,
whose only thought of time is how to waste it.
It is a healthful, refreshing exercise to combat
and put down a bold scandal—to be electrified
by a daring assertion, which you disbelieve,
and say so!—to be brightened by wit, or even
dulled by an antiquary, the only unobjection-
able resurrectionist we know of. It is healthful for the body and soul to be moved to pity,

and have sympathies put into action — it is grand to be roused to indignation, or to feel the heart leap up to meet a noble sentiment; this, indeed, it is that gives our self-esteem 'a lift,' if we have acquired the very useful habit of analysing our sensations.

Any literary-worker will give God thanks to have the winding-up of a sentence postponed, or the last line of a poem broken into fragments by the sudden presence, or happy laugh of a child. I do not mean an over-dressed, pumice-stoned child, trained, and taught, and trotted out to behave like a man or a woman of the world, but a country child, with sunshine on its face, and joy in its heart; its feet beating glad music in their unrest, and its hands full of flowers. Such a child broke one morning into Helen's room; it lived in a little white-washed cottage, covered by a primitive roof of tiles, and surmounted by a high chimney, which looked as if old Cromwell-House, hard by, had one too many, and dropped it on Dame Brooke's cottage, to get rid of it. The

cottage seemed to have grown up out of the
ground, like a mushroom ; for who would have
built a thing so small, and damp, and dreary,
in a huge cabbage-garden, from which it
was partitioned by a border of oyster-shells,
and a rampart of evil-smelling marigolds?
Helen used to say it gave her an idea of a
squatter's hut. It was crouched in the bend of
a lane, still in existence, and called 'Love-lane,'
which commenced close to Helen's residence, by
passing through three wooden posts, and then
straying on in a careless, unpremeditated sort
of way, between green hedge-rows, beneath
whose shelter the grass grew, bent and
tangled, and wild flowers flourished, until it
found itself on the verge of Kensington Road,
where its course was arrested by four posts,
placed in a perplexing manner—particularly to
stout pedestrians.   The cottage fascinated
Helen by its quaintness ; she said it gave her
ideas ; and, at last, this little child used to
peep at her through the little window of two
panes , and, after becoming acquainted with

her face, would come boldly out at the door,
and hold up its little red lips for a kiss; a
loving friendship grew and ripened between
the popular idol and the child of Love-lane.
Helen said it refreshed her to talk to it, and
to feel that it loved her *for herself*; for she
well knew that Helen Lyndsey, and Helen
Lyndsey's reputation, were things separate
and apart. She would literally punish herself
by abstaining for days from giving the child
anything, so to try its affection, and pass the
cottage in a servant's cloak and bonnet to see
if it would recognize her; but all that mat-
tered nothing to the child, it would surely
find her out and come bounding after her with
a shout and a laugh of triumphant discovery,
that was worth all the compliments of the
gorgeous ' drawing-room.'

On this particular morning it stole away
from its grand-dame, and as it came along the
lane, it filled its frock with every pretty
flower and leaf it could see in the hedge-rows;
and, watching its opportunity, entered the

house, rushed into Helen's little dressing-room
—where she was seated on her high chair at
her desk—and flung its lapfull of treasures at
her feet, exclaiming : " There, lady !"—then
blushing at its boldness, overawed perhaps, by
the presence of all around, it drew back—its
curly head seemed bent by the sunbeams that
rested on its masses of golden hair—its round,
ruddy arms were crost over its broad, white
chest, while its limbs seemed worthy to support the *Torso* of the infant Hercules.

" All for me, Benjee ?" enquired Helen, in a
voice trembling with the emotion that enriches
existence. " All those beautiful flowers for
me ?" and she gathered them up.

" And this too !" said Benjee, holding up to
her one of those mutilated glass stars which
used to adorn old-fashioned chandeliers. The
child thought that the very heart of his
offering; it had hung round his neck sus-
pended by a shred of pink tape—and he had
literally fought for it. Jimmy Dalton—the
five year old bully of Gore-lane, had wandered

so far from his home, and—attracted by its brightness, while Benjee lay on his back among the marigolds, trying to look the bright sun in the face at mid-day—endeavoured to seize it; but Benjee repulsed him so manfully that Jimmy sought refuge in roaring and flying; he now held his treasure up to Helen, with an air important yet shy—as an Indian monarch might do, if offering the Koh-i-noor to Queen Victoria.

"Look at this, dear Nobody!" exclaimed Helen, with emotion. "Is this child gifted with the terrible gift of prophecy? I have read of such. He brings this wealth of flowers—wild flowers—everyone of which I have loved and gathered, not dried, though, I never could dry a flower; I should feel like pressing out its life, in the full tide of its beauty. I should as soon think of refusing the commanded tribute of 'dust to dust,' as crushing these fair things into that foul blotting-paper! Here they are! such delicate bind-weed, white and blue!—a leaf or two of

wood-sorrel, and wild hearts-ease—a forget-
me-not, a twist of Robin-run-the-hedge, and
spires of Romping Sally!"

Her delicate fingers drew them out one
after another with tender care, and placed
them in a vase, which always waited for
flowers, by her side. "In days long past,"
she continued, "I have been inspired by every
one of these! The child, Heaven taught, has
brought them, but (now, dear Nobody, mark
and remember this, and cast that twiddling
purse aside! Note down the date. I would
we had astrologers in whom we could trust—
who would read dates as fates!)—the child
has brought me these flowers, but among
them—A FALLEN STAR! This poor, blurred,
spotted, dishonoured thing, that a magpie
would hardly pick out of the gutter, was once
what I am now—at least, in the world's eye
—a bright, particular star! I know nothing
of astronomy, but I believe stars rise, and
set, and FALL, and then—become like this!"
Leaning upon her elbow, holding it by its bit

of dirty pink tape, she balanced it between her finger and thumb—her cheeks crimson, her lips apart, her eyes burning in tears, which, if they winked, would fall; but, no, they remained wide open, staring upwards, as if she read her destiny from the motes which floated in the sunbeams; then, letting fall the glass, she crushed her hands upon her eyes with a great sob. When she looked up again, the boy was gone.

"The poor child!" she exclaimed; "I am sure I have wounded him. He came to me with his child's large heart full of generous feelings, proud of his gifts; and the gift of all others he prized, I—" She did not finish her sentence, but rolled the star up in a piece of paper, on which she had written the date, and placed it in her desk. "I gave him no thanks—no caress, though he brought me such memories! I felt, when he came in, as if a gush of mountain air crossed my brow. Surely, children are angels in disguise! And as to the omen, *he* could not help *that*." With

her usual rapidity of manner she tied on her
hat. "I must find that child and thank him."

At the instant, the servant entered. "Lady
Grant, miss," said the maid; "and her ladyship says, her ladyship came early to catch
you, miss—and won't disturb you, or detain
you, miss, only to speak a word." Helen
folded on her shawl. "And the gentleman
from the playhouse, miss—he told me to remind you he came by appointment; and,
law! miss, here's another carriage!"

"Oh, dear!" exclaimed Helen, drawing on
her gloves (she was always particular about
her gloves fitting neatly)—"Oh, dear! I did
forget him."

"And, miss, your new bonnet's come home,
and it is such a love!—shall 1 fetch it?"

Helen smiled, and paused; her hand moved
upwards to unfasten her hat ribbands. She
had always loved a new bonnet, and I saw
longed to try it on—but the child conquered.

"The bonnet can wait, Becky; and, dear
Nobody, go to those people and amuse them

until I return, I shall not be gone half-an-hour. My poor little playfellow!"

And away she tripped down the back stairs, and flew along the lane like a swallow, leaving the contents of three carriages waiting; and I would as soon have faced the Great Dragon of Wantley, if it had been in existence, as the Lady Grant, and Helen knew it; and I saw by a smile that sparkled for an instant in her eyes, that, intent as she was on the child, she appreciated my dilemma. The Lady Grant was a first-class benevolent lady of a particular mode of thinking. Her name stood conspicuous amongst the G's on every charitable committee, and no bazaar was supposed to flourish unless she 'took a stall,' which, however, was never furnished at her own expense. She patronized, in an indifferent, careless way, 'helps to the lame, and eyes to the blind,' and all manner of societies that were well-established. She dearly loved to see herself in print, but could never distinguish between fame and notoriety; and, though a

robust, strong-limbed, loud-voiced, bold-eyed
woman, she always declared she was wearing
herself out in 'the good cause,' though she
never signified what 'the good cause' was;
for the pleasure of seeing her name in type,
as belonging to these various boards of green
cloth, she paid at the rate of a guinea a-year
to each. She cut out all the advertisements
wherein she figured and placed them in a
frame, which rested on a table-easel in her
drawing-room, " to remind her," she said, " of
her duties." She had no sympathy with, or
pity for, the sorrows or sufferings of the good.
A virtuous family struggling with adversity
—a noble spirit standing against the world,
and asking no help, save of God—would be
passed over by Lady Grant as unworthy her
attention; a poor sempstress and her farthing
candle might go out together, and she would
take no note; she left such cases to the
parish and weak-minded women, who went, as
her ladyship termed it, ' muddling' about to
save useless lives and *prevent* crime. She

despised ' gentle influence,' and did not think
feeble children, or feeble women, or feeble
Christians, or feeble criminals, worth caring
for. Her calling and care were for great
criminals ; the moment she read of an atrocious
murder, or even a grand robbery, she became
exalted—she elevated her head—threw out
her chest—rang the bell to a peal, and ordered
her carriage ; her zeal mounted to boiling-
heat—she determined to convert such a case,
if not to righteousness, to Lady Grant ; and her
carriage and greys would stand for hours outside the prison-gates. If denied access to the
prisoner, she became almost frantic ; but she
had rank, reputation of a certain kind, and
wealth—so she generally carried her point ;
at all events, she always carried a black bag,
as large as a school-boy's satchel. This generally contained a petition to the king, for some
tremendous sinner's pardon, and experiences,
written by herself, of the conversions she
effected. She had worried Helen to write a
poem, befriending some great criminal, and set-

ting forth his *claims!*   As I have said, small
sinners might starve and die, or live and sin,
for aught she cared ; but to hear her talk of a
law-breaker, or life-destroyer on a large scale,
you would imagine she was commenting on
the character of Washington or Cromwell.
She regretted she had not known Nero, or
Caligula, the Borgias, or Catherine de Medicis ;
she always sighed, and said—"Think, my
friend, what converts I could have made of
them." If you ventured to say a word about
the spread of depravity, or intoxication, she
would nod her head, wave her hand, as if
chasing away a fly, and say—"Mere nothings !
—small nothings—nothings ! "   A man's beating his wife to death in those days was rather
remarkable ; but when such a case did occur,
Lady Grant was triumphant—"Such a case
to work upon !"   She had called to see if
'H. L.' had completed the poem she had certainly promised ; she spoke advisedly, but
such a theme would immortalize her—it might
some day *"be read on the scaffold!"*   The

manager came to know if the promised play
made progress, and if he could see the *dramatis
personæ* as Helen had promised, so as to
arrange the cast of characters; it was necessary to know before he made any fresh engage-
ments next season. Lady Grant eyed him
with intense contempt; her creed and caste
considered he must be a sinner, because he
was an actor; but he fell, of course, short of
her ladyship's standard : he was a large man,
but a little sinner; she did not think him
worth converting. Turning to the table, she
tumbled over the blotting-book; she found
some paper, and commenced making notes,
grumbling out bits of sentences in seeming
abstraction.

I enquired for my favourite young actress,
and heard that she was married, and left the
stage. Married two mornings ago.

" Was she likely to be happy ? "

" Yes, he hoped so ; the gentleman was
rich—had offered to pay the sum by which she
was bound to act a certain range of characters

for three years. The light business, ' Perditas,'
and ' Maria Darlingtons,' and singing comedy;
but the fates," he continued, smiling, " as 1
might remember, were against her, so he
could not honestly take the forfeiture; while
her husband could not say he bought her off.
It was her appearance the first night of *the*
play that bewitched half London; in fact, it
captivated *him*, and nearly drove Madame
mad, as she had determined on that particular conquest."

" But Madame is old."

"Not too old; ladies are *never* too old for
conquest. They have but to change the rose
of beauty for the diamond of wit; and if that
is considered too cutting, they can exchange
it for a missal—build a chapel, or endow a
saint; and so simply exchange one class of
conquest for another."

" Until the great conqueror conquers
them."

" Oh, poor Madame never dreams of that;
even when she was seriously ill, and the phy-

sician hinted that a change was possible, and she might like to make her will, she ordered him out of the room, and sent immediately for her milliner! Oh, Madame will never consider herself too old for conquest."

" But surely she is married."

The manager shrugged his shoulders.

" Did she ever contemplate poisoning her husband?" inquired Lady Grant, eagerly.

The manager looked aghast—and at the moment a bevy of ladies entered, who had been waiting in their carriage until they were out of patience.

" If she does it," persisted Lady Grant, stalking up to the manager, " I should feel obliged by your giving me the earliest information."

Her ladyship laid her card before the astounded man, and returned, with a solemn air, to the table.

The new visitors were young and charming, and delighted at finding themselves in a room with the popular actor, whose management

was the great enjoyment of London in those
play-going days. They were well-bred, and,
consequently, did not stare, or giggle, or
sneer, but looked gratified and interested,
which is particularly delightful to a middle-
aged gentleman. One had brought Helen an
offering—an embroidered handkerchief, of
such exquisite fabric and needle-work, that it
would have justified Othello's inquiries, even
if he had not been jealous! Another timidly
placed a golden paper-knife upon her table;
while a third laid a very tempting red-morocco
case beside it, with the mysterious initials
' H. L.' engraved thereon. Those girls were
all types of that fresh, pure, bright beauty
which belongs exclusively to England, and
remains the longest in bloom : the calm, self-
possessed air ; the manner, reserved but cour-
teous; the least possible consciousness of
beauty, that whispers to its possessor she cannot fail to please ; the soft, low laugh, and
gentle-speaking voice ; the hair, which at that
time fell in abundant ringlets around the full,

soft cheeks: all was very lovely! I never could look upon such like, without thanking God, and praying him to bless and keep our English girls in purity.

And then how they did speak of Helen! She had been with them to a hay-making party in the country, and enjoyed it so much; and she was so simple and unaffected, that the lady of the house would scarcely believe she was 'H. L.' They had had an authoress there once before, and she looked cold and stiff, and stately, and spoke in measured accents—slow and solemn—a minaret in motion! But, to be sure, she was an historian (the lady said), and that made a great difference. She was careful of her words, and intoned them, so that her sentences came out like a cathedral chaunt. And she was always dressed in coffee-coloured print, and had an ancient dusty look. They respected, and admired her very much at a distance; but fervently hoped she would never visit them again, for their backs ached for a week, after her departure. It seemed so necessary to sit bolt upright before her; still, she was a very superior woman—very—and so well read. She was the dread of every keeper in the British Museum. She differed almost from every other writer, and made a boast of disbelieving 'facts.' Indeed she told them, that hers was the only true history ever written! It was a great relief when she was gone. She was so artificial. Historians could not be expected to be natural, like poets. She was not at all afraid of an authoress who made hay, and gathered flowers, and romped with children, and drank milk, and had her fortune told by a gipsey, and absolutely danced one shoe off. This babble continued for some time, and I listened my very best, watching for Helen's footstep. But all this time our truant did not return. The manager was obliged to keep another appointment; the young ladies' mamma could not wait longer; and so I was charged with loves and messages —more than I could remember—and assured how glad they would be to see me, with or without H. L.

I thought of the earth that rested beneath the shadow of the rose, and was left alone with the grim Lady Grant. At last, looking up from her scribbling, she enquired, in the supercilious way which some people assume towards dependants—

"Do you live with Miss Lyndsey?"

It those days it was rude not to have added madam, or its abbreviation, to a question; but, as she commenced that style of conversation, I as rudely replied—

"No, I do not."

"Have you known her long?"

"Since her birth."

"Then, you know her father was hanged for forgery."

"I know he was not."

Lady Grant stared at me for the contradiction, which, I confess, was given most abruptly.

"You speak confidently, but I know better. I wish my calling had been certain then; I

should have converted him. He died in his
sins !"

"He lives in his sorrows," I replied, "for
he is alive—*in this house.*"

"Alive !—in this house !" she repeated.

"Yes; but such a confirmed invalid that
he never leaves his room."

"It is a very wicked, false-swearing world,"
said Lady Grant, indignantly. "I was told
that as a fact, by—a person—a gentleman,
who said he KNEW it—a gentleman—however
unconverted—of great hope, great promise.
Yes ! he may come to me yet."

Lady Grant looked so awfully mournful and
mysterious, that it seemed as if she expected
this 'gentleman' to become a *great* criminal.

"And now," she added, after a pause,
"about her mother ?"

"You will excuse me, madam," I replied,
for I was roused by her continued imperti-
nence, "but if you desire to learn all Helen
Lyndsey's family affairs, you must question
herself. She will, I daresay, tell you what
she desires to be known."

"Well, well, I daresay; I can see it *now*; the likeness—yes, there is the likeness—barely old enough. But you, madam, are her aunt—yes, her *aunt*."

I could hardly help laughing outright at this new reading, so I turned it off bitterly.

"Your ladyship must be well aware that there are secrets in all families. There is no home without its skeleton."

I have since thought how wrong it was of me, who so dreaded my own skeleton, to call up hers; for there was a terrible story about Lady Grant's husband, who was obliged to reside abroad; and I saw her, as it were, draw herself in and shudder. I cannot think how I could have been so wilfully cruel; for, after all, she was only a poor vain woman, mistaking—as my pretty maid, who in her way is a second Mrs. Malaprop, said, on another occasion—"the shadow for the substitute." Rank and fortune had failed to make her fashionable, not because of any demerits of her own, but simply because she had not enough

of either; much greater fools had achieved
high places, but then they were of undisputed
caste, or greater wealth—so as she could not
lead fashions she determined to lead criminals;
she took up conversion in one line, just as
her friend, Mrs. Crocus, took it up in another.
Lady Grant, as I have said, patronized mur-
derers—Mrs. Crocus bewailed the errors of
great opera dancers. Lady Grant sank into a
nonentity when there was no fearful criminal
under sentence of death—and Mrs. Crocus
would have been a 'nobody,' without a
first-class dancing Magdalene in her boudoir,
where ladies, some fifty years before, kept their
apes and china.

Lady Grant, as I have said would not hold
out her finger to save petty criminals—creatures
driven to robbery or the streets by starvation
were beneath her humanity; and poor shivering
ballet girls, no matter how young or unprotected,
no matter how lovely or how betrayed, might
dance through destruction to their graves, before Mrs. Crocus would present the tip of her

embroidered handkerchief to save them ; but she would summon her friends upon one pretext or another, and then impart to them the result of her good work. She would hold a 'private view' of her proselyte, and assure everyone that the open vice had become a 'veiled virtue.' And after all, self deception is so blinding, that both ladies, I dare say, believed in their charity and goodness —believed wholesale in themselves, which is the most wonderful thing of all !

This train of thought absorbed me so much for the time, that I hardly noted how closely Lady Grant was observing me. At last she rose, very civilly asked my permission to ring the bell, and desired the servant to call up her carriage.

"I see, madam, I must, like that poor benighted performer, ask *you* to prevail upon your—upon Miss Lyndsey—to let me have the poem she promised me by two, to-morrow —who knows but—"

" Someday *she* may become a *great* criminal,

and need your ladyship's benevolent assistance."

Now only fancy my saying anything so sarcastic. and dropping such a low curtsey afterwards. I could hardly believe I had been so bold.

Lady Grant stood still and stared; at last she said—

" I see, madam. you are angry, and I have to apologise for not having treated you with the respect due to the near relative of our accomplished poetess; but, madam, surely H. L.'s mother may be proud of such a daughter!"

So she departed. to spread abroad "the fact" that I was Helen's mother. These were not the days of skeleton petticoats or crinolines, and yet Lady Grant filled up the staircase; I followed her to explain her mistake, but she shook her black bag at me, and waved me off, as she did all small sinners, in utter contempt.

Quite out of temper, I was slowly returning to the drawing-room, when, looking up, there was Helen's face, all smiles and roses, peeping over the banisters.

"How could you behave so, my dear Helen? In five minutes I should have died of Lady Grant. When did you come in?"

"Before the well-bred manager departed. I so enjoyed your dilemma, it was quite dramatic; there! I saw it through the chink. Whenever I possess a house of my own, I shall have a spy closet in every reception room and listen to what my visitors say of me in my believed absence. I found my little friend pouting and crying by the post; that child is cursed with so sensitive a nature, that he will die in his teens; and so best; happy are they who die young. Having made my peace, I returned just in time to see, and yet escape, from the manager, and Lady Grant! What innocents you are! How you believe I had worked at the play, and thought of the poem, and how those dear girls (what charming girls they are) imagined I enjoyed that hay-making—never was *so* bored, or, rather, never was *more* bored in my life! I do not consider mosquitos worse than English gnats. The cream made me quite bilious; London cream will never do that."

"And did you not enjoy that country party, Helen?"

"What a question! fresh air makes me sneeze. I like it best softened with a little fog. Then I have a regard for my complexion, and an unspeakable horror of spiders, earwigs, and every insect that crawls or flies. I do not believe any grown-up young lady, emancipated from trowsers, white muslin, and a broad blue sash, could 'enjoy' syllabub, and curds and whey—not even with a lover in a straw hat and German 'blouse.'

"Then why did you pretend to enjoy it?"

"Because I like to make people happy; it helps one's popularity. Words are but air, and air is prompt payment for the trouble people take. And smiles become me better than frowns or inanity; so you see I studied their happiness, and my own good looks. I cannot afford to look discontented, or bored. I have no beauty, but brightness, and when that goes, I shall be as like a white negress, as I am in the bust that unfortunate sculptor has just finished."

She saw how pained I was by this levity.

"Well, dear NOBODY, I am done; I must not make you my mother-confessor.   You think my adaptativeness insincerity, but it does not amount to that.   I really do like to make people happy, 'not at the expense of truth,' you would say—ah! that is the old story. I am sure if I got on with truth, I should have been spared much misery; but a fact seems to me such a bare, inelegant, inartificial thing, a simple reality of pain. All pains are facts, and to me, all facts have been pains; that I think made me take refuge in fancy. Now do not look so. And yet though full of reproaches, I love to read your dear honest face."

"Oh, Helen, Helen!"

"Do not begin to preach: it was worth even one of your sermons on that plain, ugly thing, sincerity, to see the terror of our manager's look, when that strong woman talked about the poisoning—poor man! she will be his night-mare! Well, I have too faithful an instinct as to character; but I have seen more simplicity, more genuine feeling, in my limited observation of the 'green-room,' than in the usual 'run' of drawing-rooms. An actor is something like an artist. Take the one from his foot-lights, and the other from his studio, and they grope about the world like blind men in the noonday sun: they have no time for experience. An actor and an artist should have clever, worldly-managing wives; they should be left to manage their art, and their wives should manage them! That young actress and her husband can hardly be happy: my law is reversed there. But give the man of high genius an affectionate, managing wife, who can mend and make, and cut and con- trive, walk on foot when the fine-lady bride would cry for a carriage, and both will go to their graves in a hearse drawn by six black horses! I declare, I have not yet looked at my presents! When I crouched under the goose-berry-bushes, to write verses on my old slate, how proud I should have been of a copying or extract-book, bound and ruled!"

"But surely you value these offerings?"

"Oh, yes! Sometimes such gifts are purely ostentatious; the name of the donor engraved to prove an intimacy, which just now is the fashion —a registered friendship! What a pretty cas-solette! Now there comes another carriage. I must disappear. I am not at home : but, do you know, there are some who insist upon coming in, and waiting till I am disengaged— the class of people who, as Jerry says, will not take 'no for an answer,' who forget that my hours bear me a golden fruitage, and declare they will only detain me a minute, careless or ignorant of the chain of thought that minute has broken, and which it will take hours to re-unite. Editors and publishers seem to think they have *carte blanche* to intrude upon me ; but they know the value of time—at least, the value of their *own* time—so if they waste mine, I waste theirs—that is a comfort; and then there is something that increases my dignity, let me tell you, in having editors, and publishers, and managers waiting for a word! But I have got into a scrape. I promised an editor a review of a particular book—at least, he says I did. I was dancing at the time at Lady Jarvis's (the lady who wrote to request I would wear *blue stockings* at her fancy-ball), and forgot which, of two editors, I had promised, and sent it to the wrong one: everybody's talking of it! That carriage is gone, but here come two."

"Helen, why not adopt the French plan, and fix an 'at-home' day?"

"Because I should be avalanched by people who brought people; and then the people's people would bring other people; and having satisfied their curiosity, they would send more people, until I should not know a single face in my own salon. Abroad, the visitors make their bow to the lady of the house, and amuse each other; but here the unfortunate lady of

the house—no matter how overworked her
brain, or how overcharged her heart—is expected to amuse them. Besides, the most idle
of my friends would entreat to be admitted
on other days, and if I refused, accuse me of
affectation."

"Helen, you are not sincere, you like this
hero-worship—you would be miserable if you
did not create a sensation ; and what grieves
me is, that *quantity*, not *quality*, is your object.
I would rather you were a recluse by the side
of a lake, or on the top of a mountain."

She interrupted me by 'thank you,' and a
mocking curtsey.

"Helen, darling, you will never be healthy
or happy while you encourage these fevers of
mind and body ; you are fitted by nature for
higher and holier objects."

"Ah, my friend! nature pulls one way,
and art another. Would you see me in Lady
Grant's or Mrs. Crocus' line of life ? or Mrs.
Scanlan's devotional course ? Poor Mrs.
Scanlan, who will not give a farthing to the

city-mission. though she knows that, at this
moment, under the shadow of St. Paul's there
is a court, and in that court rustle and nestle
six hundred British souls who have never been
christened or married! She won't help them
out of the mire of perdition, but devotes her
gold to send abroad missionaries to turn good
heathens into bad Christians."

"Helen!"

"Nay, my dear Nobody, you cannot school
me now. Mrs. Scanlan amuses me very much,
as she herself would say, 'foreby the missionaries.' Have you observed that persons who
pique themselves upon their particular power
of observation, adopt a *pet* feature; and while
one person exclaims, 'See, *what* a mouth!'
another declares in favour of a nose, and rings
the changes upon some favourite Grecian or
Roman nose; but Mrs. Scanlan is eloquent
upon the 'eye.' Some would imagine that
we were a nation of Cyclops, having but one.
If she goes to hear a popular preacher, she
clutches me by the neck-tie, and says (always

pronouncing eye in an oily sort of way, 'oie') 'My dear, we had such a deloitful sermon; and his oie!—oh, such a oie! so blue, like. the heavens!' Or, 'Who is that lady, my dear? Did you observe the oie?' Or, 'Oh! that man—he may be a very good Christian, my dear, but he has no oie!'"

"How can you be so satirical! I am sure satire never made anyone happy."

"There! I have done, and do not talk to me about being healthy and happy. I shall never be either the one or the other. No," she added, her voice faltering, and her frame relaxing, while her cheeks grew pale, and a dew, like the damp of the grave, stood on her brow—"no, I came into the world an unwelcome guest, and knowing I should never be 'healthy or happy,' I determined to be what I am now — for a brief time. Do not grudge your poor Helen the *ignis-fatuus* which dawns before her, or the deceptive light that encircles her. I am tired now—I always am after such an overflow of words—words—words—words. And, though Jerry sleeps in my dear father's room, it is but little rest to me. I spring out in the night, thinking I hear his stick rapping against the foot of his bed, and feel so assured he has called, that I get up and listen at the door; and then I cannot resist peeping at his dear face, which looks so placid when he sleeps! But this want of rest, and this excitement, are too much for me, and it is well when I find relief in words. Pity, and pray for me !"

What could I do with her? All her life she had suffered from spasmodic attacks, brought on by excitement, and I always dreaded their coming. While some callers were shown into the drawing-room, she put her arms round my neck, as a child would, and I more than half carried her into her bed-room, and laid her upon her sofa; by that time she was white and powerless; and, as her head lay back upon the pillow, tears trickled from between her eye-lids."

"I must not have you thus," I whispered;

" you forget that I know of what will one day give you a woman's happiness."

" God help all woman-kind," she answered; " if we are only a little lower than the angels, demons rise to our level. I have often a great idea of arranging something for my sex, that would enable them to be greater workers than they have hitherto been; half the sins we commit are the fruits of unemployed power, an energy that cannot trifle with trifles, and which plunges, therefore, into what it cannot understand; we put one boy to a profession, another to a trade; another we send to toss upon the ocean; another, to make war on land; one is called to the ministry, another to the explanation, or perversion, of the law; the boy's ' bent' is discovered, and an opportunity, if possible, afforded him of following his inclination; but no matter what are the differences made by nature in girls, they must all work in the same mill, be all pumice-stoned to the same consistency, and learn all the same things.

Now, if ever I live to be a woman of influence (at present I am but a woman of note—a notoriety whom the 'next season' may look for in vain, while *débûtantes* inquire who *was* 'H. L.;' was she the same thing as Madame de Stael, or Mrs. Inchbald?)—well, if ever I am a woman of real influence, I think I would do a great deal for my own sex; I do not mean by unsexing them, because —no matter what Mary Wolstencraft says—the spheres of man and woman, and the duties of man and woman are essentially different. I do not want to argue as to which is the superior; because, in my own mind, I believe that the difference makes the equality : they are each *equal* to the duties or exertions which God and nature intended they should undertake, and one line of duty runs parallel with the other ; but there are quantities of things which would yield woman income and employment—some, perhaps, even after she had the duties of marital and maternal duties to perform : *these* are mapped out by God, in God's book, which, if I

had not read on your knee, and by poor Mary
Ryland's side, I should never have read at all!

Women could watch-make—women could
act as clerks—women would make delicious
hair-dressers; fancy the light, soft, graceful
fingers of a pretty girl, smoothing your bands,
if disposed to the severe, or curling your
tresses, if inclined to the playful—instead of
the great paw of a he hair-dresser, so heavy,
coarse, and common; women should be the
physicians of women and children—women
should never have submitted to the gross in-
fringement of the ' man-midwife !'—indeed, I
do not see why women should not be able to
do 'nothings' in our public offices as well as
men. They are expected—God help them !
—to do a great deal more, and know a great
deal more, in all educational matters, than
your great, wise professors, who spend so
many years of college-life in learning one or
two bygone things, that are very grand, and
great, and useful, I suppose, and which certainly ought to be so, to make amends for the

total want of every other species of useful or
entertaining knowledge. I fought a battle
with a very stately R. A. the other day,
who evidently considered the walls of Somerset
House as much a sanctuary as the Jews did
the holy of holies of their temple, and believed
the mystic letters insured the succession
of talent, as much as the laying on of hands
secured the apostolic; and he so civilly
sneered at female artists, that I became out-
rageous, and asked him how women could ex-
cel in Art, when they were excluded from all
the advantages that men possessed in such
abundance, and frequently failed to make use
of. I dare say he has whispered (the time
has not come for my enemies to speak out,
which, by the way, they never do until you
are down in the world) what a desperate
virago I am!

I wish women gave their thoughts more to
the social and moral condition of women. I
would not—now I am quite in earnest, and I
know the so-called social advantages and

power men possess—I would not be a man, if, with his power, I was to be weighted down with his additional responsibilities. Men are great in friendship; but every man, more or less, is a traitor in love. There, I won't . be reasoned with—go away. Why —when I have told you to go away—why will you stand there, making me talk?—I cannot help talking when anybody's by, and to-night I must be *radiant*. So give me rest, I could sleep now. Send away the people as you best can. We must make a sensation to-night; if I do not reign supreme to-night, at Mrs.——, I beg her pardon, the *honourable* Mrs. Joseph Greene's, I must be content to divide honours with Lalla Lolly Ling, a wonderful Chinese lady, who cuts watch-papers with her toes!

CHAPTER XI.

" I, oft returning from a spot
  Holy to me from many wanderings,
  Of fancy, or in fact, have felt the power
  Of melancholy stealing on my soul,
  Mingling with pleasant images, and from
  Sorrow dividing joy."

BARRY CORNWALL.

AND why had I not seen Florence? Infection might have been at first dreaded, but my illness was known to have been so purely nervous, that no such fear could have forbidden a visit to her old friend. I felt assured that some evil influence was at work, and I trusted with a mingling of indolence and pride, that time would develope truth.

I had been enquired after, and cards had been sent with the enquiries; now-a-days, little bits of printed pasteboard go out on their own account to make ' calls ;' then people thought it right to do their own visiting, so that I could not but feel I had been cruelly neglected, where I most expected sympathy and comfort.

I had not got a bit nearer the fact as to who Marley was, nor how he had got into society. He was my ever-recurring perplexity—he was the shadow over my path by day—my nightmare by night.

We all speak the same language we did some thirty years ago, go to the same churches, have the same houses of lords and commons, the same law-courts, and indulge ourselves with the notion that we are the same people ; but we are more changed during the last thirty years, than we were, during the previous century ; a movement swift, but almost imperceptible, has been sweeping away old customs and old feelings. No change can take place, and leave us exactly as it found us. We take broader views of things than we used to do; we want more space; our island seems to have grown

into a continent. I fear we are hardly as
happy as we were; I am certain we are not as
contented; we are more restless and ambi-
tious, and there seems no class of persons
without fearfully extravagant notions as
to what is right and becoming. As to the
women, one half of the female population
could be amply clothed out of the flounces
of the other half; the waste is positively
frightful! I went to a Dorcas society
the other evening, where ladies meet to make
clothing for the poor, and got so wedged in
between two crinolines on the staircase, that
I suggested it would be really benevolent
in more ways than one, to devote all surplus
drapery to 'poor clothing;' but this proposition
met no response; and one lady spoke of the
impetus trade received by increased demand,
and I got dreadfully sneered at, because I
asked if that was her husband's opinion. Still,
in some things we are greatly changed
for the better; our sympathies have ex-
tended, our charities more than doubled;
the highest class bends cheerfully and grace-

fully to instruct and improve the lowest; not only have 'the poor the gospel preached unto them,' with fidelity and zeal, but those who have the power are zealous of good works, and while one hand presents 'the book of life,' the other furnishes the food necessary for this life's sustenance. We have done great things for the improvement of the people, but not always wisely and well, and mingled with what we have done there may be rather too much of self-glorification.

Surely, we spend too much charity-money on charity dinners, when we praise each other in a way to revolt an impartial listener. Surely, we are too fond of the outward adorning of a structure, forgetting how much better it could be filled but for a display, which is rather a monument to the liberality of the founders, and the skill of the architect, than a thought for the good and comfort of the poor, who are to shelter within costly walls. All charitable institutions, hospitals, and so forth, according to my mind, should be distinguished by their plainness and simplicity; but with all my fault-finding—and it is strange that although I am considered a tolerably cheerful 'nobody,' my experiences, as I have noted them down, are not often written with a sunbeam—but with all my fault-finding that money is needlessly expended on the exterior decorations of our buildings for charities, there is one knowledge that fills me with gladness, such as I might feel if an angel's wing wafted a pure breath from heaven, into my soul; it is—that all these mighty structures were in men's hearts, before one stone was laid upon another; thousands added brick to brick, and comfort to comfort in these buildings, whose names can never be heard, in association with them. Thousands of pennies and shillings have been toiled for, and taken from the absolute necessaries of life, by earnest, thoughtful Samaritans, whose ministering mite is of more value in the 'great Father's' book of immortality, than the 'ten-pound—third donation' of the millionaire, which draws down such crashing applause from pompous men, who get up self-glorifying dinners at great taverns.

There is nothing in this mighty London that moves me more, than the inscription so frequent on our finest institutions, 'Supported by Voluntary Subscriptions;' other countries may talk of what their government does—we know and feel what our people do!

Oh those million pennies of the poor are golden sands, in the great account of human virtue!

The increased and increasing sympathy is more blessed to the giver than to the receiver, —whatever opens the heart is good—and the cheerful giver has a perpetual feast.

We never hear of a 'new charity' without wondering it was not thought of before—so much it was needed; in all this we are improved,—and though Mrs. Jackson, whose husband had but two-hundred-a-year, would give a pound a year to the ' Hampstead Dorcas Society," because Mrs. Bell, with an income of eight-hundred-a-year, gives a pound; still, the effect, even of charities such as these, is to augment our national benevolence. But, to me, one of the strange things of my time, is, that the reign of wit and poetry being past, we have become a 'fast' nation—we steam and telegraph the whole world. I do not understand how it is, or why in our old age, we should grow so desperately active, I do not quite like it:—The electric telegraph seems to me a wizard, a sort of Michael Scott in the mercantile and shipping interests. I would much rather not enter his den, to send a message to the great Mogul, and get an answer in a quarter-of-an-hour; and I often wonder what the old man of the sea will think of gutta percha tubing. I do not want to know at what hour my friend breakfasted in New York; and little thought I should live to see the time when England should become a bulky sort of Ariel, and—

"Put a girdle round about the world!"

in something less than "forty-minutes."

I may ponder and wonder at the miraculous movements of the past thirty years, but that which causes me most concern, is the uncertainty—the unsoundness—the instability—the puff-ball of society—as it now is. A new element seems to have been created, in which a new class of persons exist—a demon, armed with ten-fold power, has entered, been believed in, welcomed, cherished—even in our virtuous village homes. Mississipi schemes and South Sea Bubbles came and went, and left the people fevered and feeble; but they were not half so bad as living amid a population infected, diseased, festering absolutely with a disease which seems to grow by what it feeds on. Society, from the highest to the lowest, is unsound. There are hundreds of well-dressed, and tolerably well-bred, flimsily-educated people in circulation amongst us, of whom we know nothing, but that judging from the display they make, they must be rich; and upon this plea we admit them into the sanctuary of our homes—a brougham comes to

tea—a clarence and pair to dinner—and why?
—we believe them to have money!—money
is everything—money, a motive—money, a
reward—money, the hope—money, thrusting
vulgarity into high places—money, taking the
time-honoured seat of eloquence and patriotism
in our senate—money, casting the spoil of
widows' houses, and the orphans' dowry, from
the platform of so-called religious meetings
into the mouths of a gaping multitude, who,
because of his money-repute, exalt the horn of
the hypocrite and bow the knee to Baal!
Money thrusts its griping hand into all things.
It has poisoned the well-springs of life and
honour; it has made the noble, of spotless
descent for twice two hundred years, forget
the duty he owed to an unsullied line of an-
cestry, and sit at the gold-covered board of
the grovelling and shameless speculator; it
extorts the lowest bows and the finest compliments; it is not a pestilence confined to a
particular locality, but its trail is over our
land and our colonies; those who have it, grow

insolent in its strength; and those who have it not, assume its insolence, and involve hundreds in ruin by a fiction.

I am a peaceable-mannered old body as can be, and my burning thoughts consume only myself; but I cannot restrain my indignation when I see the bubbles that never would have escaped from the wash-hand basin which cradled their birth, but that they have the reputation of 'making money.'   Hero-worship sanctifies the worshipper, but this mammon-worship!—I often blush for England, I can hardly recognize it as the calm, sustaining, dignified, glorious England of the long war; we worshipped glory then; we had our kings of the battle-field, and our monarchs of the ocean; we had poets worthy to hymn their praises, and many marvellous men in science and in art; we have great men still among us— great, noble men—who carry the name of England honourably throughout the world; and yet mere dust and shovel-men are as much thought of in society, simply because,

with an alchemy, born of sin, they turn their
dust to gold.   Oh! at many of our " enter-
tainments," now-a-days, you have a fair
chance of being handed or *armed* down to
dinner by a gentlemanly swindler, whose next
repast will be eaten in Newgate.

Gambling, some thirty years ago, was chiefly
confined to cards and dice ; and, when it was
whispered to me that Marley was a gambler,
I understood by it simply that he played more
than he should at cards.

Now-a-days, who *has not* gambled on the
Stock Exchange, or in shares ?—or—but why
do I so ramble ?—I ought to write only of
the past, but I feel impelled to pen my
simple protest, that, with all our utilitarian
views, and all our wide-spread philanthropy,
the mammon-worship, under some guise or
other, sweeps all that is high-toned before
it ; the Moloch of our system demands
human sacrifice ; it immolates its victims by
countless thousands, to gratify a lust for
gold, and a passion for display.

And—yet—I fear I have not given the 'honour to whom honour is due,' in the method and manner of our public charities.

I remember that Helen, like all who come prominently before the public, was greatly tormented, not only by invitations and albums, but by circulars, begging-letters, and beggars of all kinds, from the 'genteel beggar' to the beggar of the streets. There was not a charitable institution in England, I believe, which did not send her a printed statement of the good it had done, and the good it hoped to do,—with her assistance; there was not a church that needed repair, or rebuilding, or restoration, of which the rector neglected to forward a 'statement' to 'H. L.' Begging-letter impostors of course singled her out, at once; and distressed 'parties' requiring loans, fell upon her without consideration or mercy; schools attacked her so vigorously, that she was quite horrified at the ignorance of the past, and bewildered by the educational advantages promised to present and future,

generations; indeed, she used to say intellect
seemed to make such progress, that the poorer
classes would be well prepared for everything
but *work*. From the number of widows who
appealed to her sympathy and generosity, it
might have been imagined the husbands of
England had been smitten by the plague, had
not petitions from whole families of orphans suggested that the *parents* of England must have
been swept from the face of earth by some
dire calamity. There is a deplorable want of
common sense, as well as delicacy, in these
appeals to public characters; I have been
both distressed and ashamed at the wholesale beggary practised in England against
strangers—singers or actors, or any class of
persons, who, after years of hard and expensive labour—years of struggle and obscurity
—at length achieve the object of their lives;
and, for a brief time, have the opportunity of
providing for the present and the future, by
the growth and ripening of the seed they
have sown with their own hands. It has been
my privilege, since my entrance to the green

room with Helen's play, to know several of
the most distinguished *artistes*—distinguished
by their talent—distinguished by their private
moral worth, and remarkable for their child-
like simplicity; their hearts are always sus-
ceptible, their hands open, and I do not
hesitate to say, their charities are triple
the charities of those who *inherit* the wealth
which they, by their labour, gain. They are
continually giving their money, or what is
their money—their talent and their time; it is
humiliating to know they are perpetually appealed to for charities—the charities that
we of England are bound by every law, human
and divine, to uphold and protect, *ourselves ;*
yet we are mean enough to rush, like
a pauper people, upon any foreigner whose
talent buys our gold, and ask back earnings
which are earned by hard and anxious labour;
because, before they can earn, as I have said,
they pass through years of struggle, obscurity,
and expense ; while their harvest is uncertain,
and, at best, of short duration.

And then, young authors forwarded such pyramids of manuscript, entreating her to read them first, and then prevail upon some influential publisher to give them to the world.

Poor Helen! these young creatures moved more frequently by a taste, than a genius, for literary pursuits, always awoke her sympathy; it was marvellous the excuses she made for rubbish that would have degraded the Minerva press; and she got into a labyrinth of scrapes by the geniality and gentleness of her replies. However much she enjoyed a little mischievous tormenting, her fellow feeling for those who desired to improve their condition 'by sweat of brain' was so earnest, that she became calm and serious the moment such an appeal was made. I have seen her shed tears of vexation over a stupid story or a most unhappily bad poem, because she knew what the disappointed author must feel; and 'unfit for publication' was an opinion she could never bring herself to write; but this sympathy and generosity was productive of evil—she excited hopes which never could be fulfilled, and laid herself open to the charge of insincerity!

Several female boards of green cloth requested her to accept a place as 'lady-patroness,' or 'member of committee.' She was entreated to hold plates at charity sermons— to choose any 'stall' at the then new-born bazaars, if she would only preside at one ; to 'christen' yachts, and to lay foundation stones.

A little flattered by all this popularity, she began by giving five pounds in furtherance of some missionary object ; and a week afterwards, at least half-a-dozen other 'sects' assured her, unless she gave also to them, she would be set down as belonging to the 'opposite' party. Poor Helen! if she had continued her liberality, every pound she received should have been five times doubled.

Poor girl! she used sometimes to get irritable and petulant under these inflictions, but more frequently regretful that she could do so little ; and her feelings were, at times, ter-

ribly tried. All her life, as I have said, she
had been passionately fond of children ; and
this fondness continued amid all the distract-
ing circumstances of her brilliant public career.
She had been induced to give the sanction of
her name to a juvenile reformatory, and took
the deepest interest in its proceedings.

I made an observation, one day—when I
knew how much she was pressed for time,
and still saw how anxious she was to attend
the usual meeting of the ladies' committee—
to the effect that it was one thing for fine
ladies to give the glory of their names to an
institution, and another to work for it ; and
she turned upon me, as she would always do,
when she thought I had been unjust, with a
proof of my injustice.

"You are," she said, "like the malcon-
tents in this and every other country—judging from what you hear, not from what you
see. Now, my dear Nobody, how do you
know that the ladies of our committee do not
work ? What proof have you that they are a

set of titled idlers, who do nothing but sleep
in the mornings, and dress and read novels—
(by-the-bye, we who write should be the
last to find fault with those who read)—
who, moreover, tyrannize over their maids,
snub their husbands, neglect their children,
and have no sympathies with the poor? That
is the true revolutionary reading of the word
'lady,' is it not? Was there ever a country,
my dear friend, where the idle-nothings, and
do-nothings, did not raise a cry against the
have-somethings, and do-somethings? It
would be so delightful for those who inherit
rags, ignorance, and discontent, to have a
'share and share alike' law, that would give
them clothes, and food, and knowledge, and
render them 'respectable' at once. Now look,
I would reform, not by drawing any down, but
by raising many up; and that is what the
aristocracy and gentry of England are labour-
ing to do—heart and soul. I see it, and hear
it, and all England will know it, before another
quarter of a century is passed. 'It is meet

right, and their bounden duty so to do."
Granted. *But they are* doing it. Who found
and support charities? Who clothe and
educate, and visit, and enlighten? The right
minded, truth-seeking 'high and upper classes'
those classes who supply the vital strength of
the country. Surely, the poor have no power
of themselves, to furnish homes, and build and
endow schools and hospitals; yet it is done
for them. I know there is a host of malcon-
tents, of the Thistlewood family, who would
beat down in England, what it has taken
centuries of good English flesh and blood—
hands and hearts and heads—to build up;
who labour hard to find out, or to make,
a grievance, and gloat over it, as over a new
pleasure; who having no sympathy with what
is right, shout 'to the echo' when they
discover a wrong. They have their Scribes
too, sharp-eyed, sharp-tongued, steel-pen men,
who, because they have no appreciation for the
beautiful, or high, or holy, revel in reviling,
and instead of drawing the classes together,
so as to form a self-helping whole, without

endangering any, seek to divide, so as thus to conquer, for their own base purposes. One of these fellows, keen as a rat, bitter as henbane, made it his boast some few years ago, that by a blast of his penny whistle, he would overthrow the aristocracy of England!

"God be thanked! they live, notwithstanding, in the hearts and minds of the people; who have learned, in spite of many such teachers, that the best friends of the poor are the rich; and that the high-born are the truest and safest props of the lowly.

"There, I have been like that woman in the new song:—

"What a pity, when charming women
Talk of things that they don't understand."

"Now, you shall come with me to-day, and note facts. And as to my time? Change of occupation is the best rest. There will be abundant leisure for rest to this listless and inert body in the grave! Did you say, 'That is a gloomy idea?' No! I do not think so, by any means. I do not think the Immortal Spirit which moves us by its

influence ever intended us to be still. It is
this earthly tabernacle, this quagmire of flesh
and blood, that keeps whining for ' rest.'   I
have very little time, as you have just said,
to bestow upon this ' ladies' committee,' the
only one I really belong to; for I think a
woman cannot be complimented when asked
for the influence of her *name*—as if her *name*
had nought to do with herself, and her mental
powers went for nothing.   If such a request
were put into plain English, it would just
signify—' Madam, will you be a decoy duck ?'
So I have given up the others; but I
like this Reformatory; it approaches what
my soul longs to do, but dare not—to go
into the highways, and woo the outcasts of
my own sex to reformation.   When I am
old and ugly, *that* shall be my work!
God help me!   I can easily promise that,
for I shall never be old.   Now, do not talk
nonsense, my dear Nobody.   The sword is
wearing out the scabbard; but our lives should
be calculated by deeds, not days.

"I have a theory—or a dream—which is it?

Are dreams theories, or theories dreams?
Well, I have a faith flitting in and out of my
mind—at one time threatening to become
established, and take possession of me: at
other times, shooting through my brain, with
the brightness and rapidity of a sun-beam—it
is this—that all the really good things we
intended to do while in life, and have been
prevented from accomplishing by death, we
shall be permitted to achieve in some future
state.

"Now do not contradict me. I am certain
nothing that is good is ever lost! You believe
that? Well, good thoughts, though not
immediately carried into action, are like the
seeds of the thistle-down, winged and wafted
somewhere, or someway, to fructify, if not in
the parent brain, in some other brain; whether
this be by an invisible, spiritual agency, in which
we are netted by Divine will, or by the pro-
cess of development, I cannot tell; and there
is no use in my thinking it over, for I should
never find it out; but so I am certain it is;

thus, when I conceive a good thought, I bless God, for I know it will make wings unto itself, and spread; and if I cannot work it out, either I shall be permitted to do so in another state, or some one else will do it for me.

"Whenever a selfish person exclaims, when something considered a new idea (of new ideas there are very few) comes before the world, 'What right has so and so to *that?* that is *my* thunder,' I feel inclined to exclaim, more than a lady should. But oh! it is not worth while to do so; the mind that goes floundering through the shallows, in perfect contentment if it can but see its own reflection, is not worthy of being pushed into deep waters."

"But, Helen, surely there is nothing more mean or dishonest, than adopting other people's ideas, and giving them forth to the world as your own."

"Oh, those brain-pickers are dreadful creatures; you find them at the bottom of dinner-tables, or in sly corners of rooms, and men say they frequent the gloomiest tables at

the clubs, and the omnibus-box at the opera, and
they hunt up the newspaper people, and are
down upon knee to all kinds of editors, turning a penny in retail literature, winking like
owls in honest day-light, and practising
their picking and stealing in the dark.
It is almost enough to make a lady, if she be
an authoress, swear! You do not know how
I am robbed. I don't care about their taking
my printed ideas, because one day that will
be discovered; but I know that same eager-
eyed, long-faced, distorted penman, who
does not let his charity and love for 'the
people' abate his creature comforts, and
loves to revel, almost as well as to stab—
will catch my little butterfly society
thoughts, and produce them minus the delicate down, the rose-tinting, which is, after all,
their only attraction, and then float them
about, all ragged, and torn, and tattered,—
the wretch! And only fancy, if I do
produce a little witty thing, having it
shattered into worthless splinters, by the

clumsy fingering of a diner-out! It is
worse than having your best dress spoiled
by an imperfectly-developed dress-maker, or
your pet ringlet, which has cost you a quire of
curl-paper to instruct in the curl natural,
bronzed and frizzed by the over-heated tongs
of a hair-dresser. When my hair is quite
white, I shall fold it in one huge curl round
my face, and place over it a Mary Stuart cap,
of the most delicate Mecklin lace, crowning
the erection by a bewitching old-lady hood,
of violet satin, softened by black Brussels
lace, tied under my little chin with a soft, rich
bow of wide violet French satin ribbon ; *that*
will suit my complexion. I do not so much
mind wrinkles; but I vow I will never submit
to be yellow and colourless. I'll enamel
first ! I wonder you do not exclaim—'oh,
Helen !' which I understand as a mark of
strong disapprobation."

And so she would rattle on at times, in her
wildest or most wayward of moods, still leaving me something to think over; while at

others we would drive together, or sit to·
gether for hours, and she would never speak;
this was not the case in society; she was always light and brilliant there; when at her
desk, she was sufficiently concentrated to
gratify the strictest disciplinarian; but with
me, she never thought it necessary to keep to
· a subject a word longer than she liked, fluttering on or folding her wings just as she
desired.

We drove on for some time, and at last she
exclaimed—

"Now here we are! there is the countess
getting out of a hack-carriage, in her little
poke beaver bonnet. I call her a glorious
woman; no matter what her duties at the
Palace are, she finds time to investigate cases
of distress with her own deep-seeing eyes. I
think she could guide you while blind-folded
through the most fearful lanes in Westminster.
She comes to us with terrible stories of misery
and destitution; and when she heaps case
upon case, and we wonder if the funds of the

institution will be able to relieve *all*, behold, it is all done! She seems to me to have large funds of her own, and commands other people's; no one refuses of whom she asks, for she knows who to ask—there, this is our board-room door."

Helen introduced me as the 'friend who had given a large donation' (she thought it large, and it was so for me); and, in her own quaint, playful way, satisfied the ladies that I was quite to be trusted; and, therefore, I sat in a corner and listened to my heart's content.

Case after case was brought forward, not only by the countess 'in the little poke beaver bonnet,' but by all the ladies, with a zeal and earnestness which left no doubt of their desire to do good. And I do not know that I was more struck by *that*, than by the business tact and precision with which they conducted their quiet unostentatious meeting. Every item of cost and expenditure was carefully noted and compared; the matron was

sent for and questioned; and then we all
visited the kitchens and dormitories; and,
finally, examined the young creatures who
were here trained in a new life. We saw
several of their relatives, who, under certain
restrictions, were permitted to visit them, and
nothing could exceed their expressions of
gratitude. There was one weeping mother,
who knew that her son's deviation from
honesty could be traced to his own father;
and it was touching to see how she endeavoured to shelter her husband, and still
excuse her child. Helen wept with her; and,
indeed, all who were present were deeply
affected.

There was not too much preaching, and
very little self-glorification—which, however,
will creep into 'the best regulated families;' I
fear it is a part of human nature;—but, while
the past was set aside as something too painful to remember, the future was held up
as full of hope, respectability, comfort—even
prosperity.

The world need not be told of the labours of such 'good samaritans ;' the printed lists of all our useful and needful 'societies' afford conclusive evidence that the most earnest of the 'workers' are those who might, if they pleased, find ready excuses why they should not let

> "The clamorous voice of woe
> Intrude upon the ear;"

why they should minister only by deputy to 'the sad varieties of woe;' and why they should be released from toil by employing subordinates to do the work of healing— to body and to soul !

CHAPTER XII.

'Long from a country even hardly used,
  At random censured, wantonly abused,
  Have Britons drawn the shape with no kind view,
  And judg'd the many by the rascal few.'

CHURCHILL.

HELEN'S generosity always bounded forward to make amends for injustice or irritability; and, as I have intimated, she lost no time in admitting Jerry to the presence of his master.

She suffered him to enter the room while her father slept, and had the satisfaction to see something like the old kind smile tremble on his lips, when his eyes, after wandering

T 2

round and round the room, at last rested upon
Jerry. He beckoned Jerry to him; and the
Irishman knelt as he drew near the chair.
Mr. Lyndsey passed his hand over the face,
and along the arm, caressingly, as if feeling
something he knew; then smiled, while his
lips moved, as if seeking a word, and his old
servant murmured—

" Jerry, yer honour."

Surely the mysterious spirit returned to
its shattered dwelling at that moment; looking on the brown, rugged, and wrinkled face,
so devoid of beauty, and yet so earnest and
devoted in its expression, he muttered—

" Jerry—poor Jerry !—where is Helen ? "

Helen was standing before him, with clasped
hands and lips apart, hoping that once again
—if only once—he might recognize her.
But no; he smiled faintly, and moved his
head, with the courtesy which never forsook
him, as if she had been a strange lady.

Without again acknowledging the presence
of his ' follower,' Mr. Lyndsey seemed gratified

by his presence, took the food and medicine,
which Helen herself had always administered, as
freely from Jerry as from her; and afterwards,
if at all restless, Jerry managed to tranquilize
him by 'croning' over one of his old songs,
which invariably arrested his attention, and
to which he would keep time by a movemen
of his foot or hand : to Helen this was a grea
relief. The poor Irishman had that enduring,
loving spirit which could 'bear all things.'
Although acute and cunning, Jerry was always
deficient in what is called common sense; but
as this has very little to do with affection—
the deep-rooted affection of an earnest nature
—there, at all events, the want was not felt.
Helen told me, that, if she did not watch him,
she believed he would live upon air; for he
would not leave his master to dine with the
servants, and he deemed it disrespectful to
eat in his master's room. The utmost Helen
could prevail on him to do, was to take some
food outside the door, where it was left on a
marble table, which stood on the landing.

When Mr. Lyndsey was sleeping as tranquilly as an infant, and Jerry, leaving the door ajar, had crept into the lobby to partake of the refreshment, which Helen had placed for him with her own hands—(the lobby window looked up the lane, and the broad leaves of a large magnolia shaded the staircase from the sun)— I often sat on an old-fashioned seat placed in its recess; and there poor Jerry would whisper me news of his master.

" Sure its the greatest of earth's mercies," the poor fellow said to me, " that something— the Lord above knows what it is, for I don't— gives me power over him—him, that ought to have the power of the world over me and mine. This power makes him take anything from my hand, all as one as if it was offered him by Miss Helen, the darling. And if he is fretful, or restless, I just begin a line or so of ' Jockey to the fair,' or 'Benbow,' or 'On board of the *Arethusa*,' or a tune, he was mighty fond of entirely ' long ago,' something he used to whistle himself, and which he larned in

furrin parts, when both of us, master and
man, had more life in 'em, than they'll ever
have again in this world.   If he's ever so
restless, I just come over two or three bars
of that, and he gets as quiet as a sick lamb,
and falls off asleep."

"Miss Helen says she thinks *you* never sleep,
Jerry."

"That's just her fancy. I'm in a sort of slumber half the time; she needn't fear; all my life
I took great comfort entirely out of the sleep. .
Oh, sure it is the wonder of the world for re-
lieving the body of its troubles; and waking
after a good night's rest, with the glory of the
Lord's sunshine on me, I never could help falling down on my two bare knees, no matter
what work was before me, in gratitude to
Almighty God for the sweetness of that rest.
The sleep's a wonderful thing, and there's
nothing I ever heerd tell of, we could put in
the place of it; only there's something *in us*, it
never comes over.   Often and often, if any
of them English grooms, came up to the hay-

loft, I was glad to make a home of, and saw
me sleeping, they might think me nothing but
a bundle of rags ! May be at that very minute,
the *something*, that is me, and isn't me, would
be, in my far-away home—ay, indeed, in Ireland—listening to the birds singing, and the
river rowling, and seeing pleasant faces, that
have been shining, plase God, among the Saints
in Heaven ! long ever ago, and hearing voices,
that will never again make sweet music in
this world ! Sure, it's well to have pleasant
times in our sleep, if we can't have them when
we're awake; only, they fade like a flash of
lightning. But sure everything does the
same — here to-day, and gone to-morrow !
Oh, I sleep well ! any where, any way; one
eye on the master, the other shut; and they
take it turn about. If it wasn't for him, dear
gentleman, though he's so altogether out of
himself now, it's not even the remains of
an eye I'd have in my head, good or bad.
Sure, I've no right to my own body, or
limbs, or voice, or anything; the soul

that's in me, never was my own, I believe.
I never could come rightly to the knowledge
of it; but, from all I gather, I don't think
I've any right to meddle with it,—because,
though it dwells in me, it has to return to Him
who sent it; I heard that from the best authority, so I'm not going to forget myself as a
Christian (though it's far from a true one I am),
and say Mr. Lyndsey has a right to my soul,
though it's small good it would do him if he
had; but a right to every bone in my body,
to every bit of me, dead or alive, he certainly
has; and I only wish I could make a *raal*
sacrifice of myself, for his sake, and it's happy
I'd be to lay down my head on the block—
ay, would I—even without benefit of Clargy,
if it would do him any good. Oh, ma'am
dear! isn't it woeful, when yer heart's with
any one—when yer whole desire, by night
and day, is to do something out of the way
entirely, so that the loss of an arm, or an eye,
or a leg, or anything for their sakes, would be
a comfort—isn't it like breaking every bone in

yer body—isn't it like drawing away yer heart's blood to know and feel, and see that you can do nothing for them of any account— only must walk quietly on to the grave, feeling that the sooner ye'r there, the better, for ye'r no good in the wide world to any one or any thing."

"Jerry, that is not your case; in your humble way, you have been useful and faithful, —faithful beyond all price."

"God bless you, ma'am! God bless you for your kind thought! I've been *silent,* any way— may be, too silent—silent for the sake of one, and not thinking of others; but sure, at the last day, I'll be judged by the light I have, not by the light given to other people! God help us, we're all sinners! and the greatest of all mercies is to have time given us for repentence—*that is* a mercy; but, for Mr. Lyndsey (heaven be his bed!), I shouldn't have had *that.*"

"How was it, Jerry?"

"And you don't know it! Well, that is

queer, too. I'll see if the master is sleeping still; and if he is, as Miss Helen's out—if yer honour will just sit quiet there, where the broad green leaves of that fine tree make a pleasant shade, and I can hear if *he* stirs—I'll tell you; and then judge, if I'm not bound hand and foot to the master, the same as if I was a *nagre*—born black—a nataral collar round my neck, full of spikes, which I've heerd they all have.—Praise the Lord for not putting it on the poor Irish, who have enough to bear without it."

, Jerry entered on tip-toe, with that strangely balanced gait, which frequently made us think he must stumble; but he kept firm enough, crossing one foot before the other.

"He's as sound as a rock," he said, returning; "and that's a quare saying, for rocks are unsound enough sometimes."

I sat down on the window-seat, and Jerry, placing one hand on the marble slab, and resting one foot on the instep of the other, passed his hand, in a deliberate way, over and over

his face, and commenced in that low-toned
whisper in which he constantly spoke, when
he had anything to communicate which required secrecy, and poor Jerry had a great
love for the mysterious.

"Can ye tell me, if it'll ever be made clear
to us when the Lord thinks fit to dim the
senses in a poor body, so that while the eyes
are open, and everything going on, the eyes
don't see, and the ears don't hear, and there's
no understanding. And yet, as I said awhile
ago, when the eyes are closed in sleep, I could
take my Bible oath that them senses are away,
maybe, in the pleasant fields of youth, or out
boating on the sea, or a-horseback, following
the hounds — or, maybe, up in the skies,
among the angels. Might it be, I wonder,
under the beams of the Lord's own smile—"

"How do you know that this is the case,
Jerry?"

"Well, besides my own drames, I'll tell
you. In sleep, the master often comes to
himself; the ould kind look is back on his

face; the turn of his head is the same, and
he murmurs words in his sleep that never
passed his lips for years. Don't I know?
Maybe, I don't! God look down on us all,
and forgive us all our sins. Amen. Only,
another thing has come to me; setting a case
anyone's ill, the doctor is sent for at once,
and the sickness is talked over, and it's all
open, and everything done for it—that is, unless it has something to do with the brain.
If a lady or gentleman's touched in the head,
there is such a hiding of it, and such a mystery made of it, as if it was a sin or a shame;
when I know, as well as anyone that ever broke
the world's bread (and hard as a paving stone
it is, sometimes), that if it was taken kindly
and openly in hand at once, and not pushed
into a hole and corner, and hunted away as if
it was a plague or a pestilence, it could be
seen to and cured, like anything else; for the
Almighty sends us a cure for everything.
Just to think of people being ashamed to own
the thrials sent them for their good! If any-

one with knowledge had watched the poor
masther at first, it's not there he'd be this
blessed Sunday evening, with no sense left
him but in his dreams! And sure he'd be
proud of Miss Helen; though he'd have the
terror over him still."

"What terror, Jerry?"

The poor fellow looked alarmed for a moment, and then added, " The terror, maybe,
of his wife upsetting him."

"You forget, good Jerry. I thought everyone knew that Mrs. Lyndsey is believed to.
have been dead these two years; that her income, whatever it really was, died with her.
Surely you remember our speaking of it ?"

"Ay, bedad! ma'am, sure enough; and
as to her income dying with her, it was dead
while she lived! for sorra a good it ever did
to anyone! She hated the sight of me;
and, what was worse, she hated the sight of
her own child. Sure it's quare things we see
in this world! and yet, poor woman, my
heart often ached for her."

"But about yourself, Jerry?"

"Bedad, it's mighty strange, entirely, for me to stand here in pace and quietness, looking at the dancing of them sunbeams—straight lines they may be, for anything I know to the contrairy—from the Almighty's throne; and maybe, it's messages they bring from heaven, though I can't read 'em; and yet here am I, that never thought to reach England's ground, anyhow; and the way of it was this: I was born, bred and reared, until I was a well-grown slip of a gorsoon as ever drew a moon-light salmon out of the New Ross River, a little below a place ye might have heerd tell of, they call it by the name of Inistigue, the wild, lovely woods and walks are there, and the river keeps wandering about the country, from where a great foreign lady, one Rose Macrue founded the town of New Ross, falling herself from off the scaffolding of the church she was building to the honour of the holy Virgin Mary; only seeing that if she came to the ground, she'd be disfigured for life, the

angels took her to glory, before ever she
touched earth, and so carried her right up to
heaven; and what the people found below, all
of a heap, wasn't the Lady Rose Macrue at all,
only some make-believe, which they buried in
the church, where you may see her image
to this day.   Well, it was about there. I
spent my time, divartin' meeself, and knowing
little, only beginning to *go to my duty*—that
is confession, you understand—and doing a
hand's turn for anybody that wanted it—
especially for Madame Butler's horses—with a
heart and a half, and wearing my shamrock of
a St. Patrick's day, in spite of the Orangemen
(this was before the turn of the 98) ; and just
as if the blessed saints had a hand in me,
Mr. Lyndsey came to Ireland on a visit to his
gran'-aunt—a fine ould lady, one of an ancient
race—a Butler; yes, indeed, his gran'-aunt
was a Butler, an Ormond Butler; the blood
of the rale Butlers was so thick, you could cut
it with a knife; and it's little she ever thought
any of that blood, let alone her own sister's

son, would be thramping to the city London,
and taking up with a parcel of white nagurs,
that would sell their souls for gold; but that's
neither here nor there; the good red drop
was in the whole generation—only, to be
sure, it grows waker and waker as time goes
on. Well, ma'am, her honour kept a sort of
open house—the doors war' there, to be sure,
but they war' never shut against anything but
winther and hard weather; and even then, the
touch of a beggar's finger would push them
open : she was what we call a black Protestant
herself—oh, she was Church and State to the
backbone! yet she never asked a *poor* man
what his religion was, though, I'm sorry to
say, that a *rich* Roman never crossed the door-
step. Well, Mr. Lyndsey—Masther Arthur
we called him then—came, sure enough; but
I own I was sorry to see him in a red coat,
and the red coats are born enemies to my poor
counthry, and the love for it was warm in
my heart, as it was in the heart of every united
Irishman. God help them ! the poor boys did

not look for anything, barring the good of their
counthry, and trusted to their shupariors to
show them how to bring it about.

"Masther Arthur often took me out with
him, when he went shooting in the groves of
Woodstock; and sometimes he'd wear his un-
dress uniform, which his aunt gloried to see
him in. He was only a slip, about seventeen
—maybe not so much; but, to see him as
you used to see him on the Heath, you'd
never have known him to be the same.
There's times now, when he turns his head in
that soft sleep, that he's more like what he
was then—than ever he looked since you
knew him. Well, the rage of the country
then, agin' the *red*, was as bad as a mad
bull's, and I didn't like him to be going out
in it, and I tould him so. 'They'll be shooting at ye, sir,' I says, by way of a half joke,
as we were wandering on together—'all as
one, as you do be shooting at the birds; and
it would break your honourable gran-aunt's

heart to have a drop of the blood of the Butlers spilt on the soil that owes them so much,' I says. 'And lave the jacket at home,' I says."

" 'Would *you* try to save me, Jerry?' he says.

" 'Is it would I? Could I help it, yer honour, setting a case I was murdered with the same stones, or the same shot!'

" 'And if you could not save me, Jerry, would you give information?' he says again.

" 'Indeed, then, sir,' I says, 'I would not; I would not turn informer to save myself from destruction; I couldn't tell.'

" Well, he argued the point on and on with me; but, in course, being a Saxon, he couldn't see my rayson; and we war coming through the tangle of the wood, and as we war turning home, just rounding a corner, I saw the muzzle of a gun covering my poor fellow, and at the same minute I heard the full roll of laughter come from below the bank; and I

knew that it was some of Masther Arthur's
friends, who would be with us in a minute.
But that minute would cost my darlint young
masther his life; so I says, quick as light,
'Stop, yer honour, look there! What's that,
sir?' trying to turn him out of the danger; a
minute would do it. But he walked on study-
like. The gun covered him as neat as if he was
nothing but a thrush! I saw it, and I knew the
hand that would pull the trigger. I felt it was
all up with the fine young gentleman; and, seeing there was nothing else for it, 'By yer
lave,' I says, and I knocks him down; and,
as I did, bang went the gun, and down I fell
a-top of him. I was hit in the shoulder—
winged. In a minute his friends were round
us. Such a scrimmage as it was! and they
driving at me, as if *I* had done it. 'Hould
hard!' shouted the darlint—'hould hard!'
He saved me. 'My poor, faithful Jerry, God
bless you! I *saw the aim myself*—but too
late, only for you! 'Now, my friends for a

chase; the cowardly rascal can't have escaped;' and they opened a view halloo, as if the hounds were unkenneled. Of course, they couldn't find him."

"Jerry! I fear you know where he was concealed."

"To be sure I did. I was as close to him as I am to you."

"But Jerry!"

"Ah then, let me alone. I ask your pardon, but if you want to rayson that I should have tould, it's no use. We had as good a right to make laws for ourselves, as the Saxons had to make them for us! and I can't go on, if you begin to work away at the reason and the right, which we can't see the same way; as you know yerself, the Irish and English can never ride on the same side of the car."

"Well, go on."

"That poor gentleman rode twenty miles that day, to bring me the finest doctors on

Ireland's ground; and they used to have me
in to show me to the company, and indeed,
it's many a drop 'too much they gave me
afther dinner, until the big mistress forbid it,
because of the inflammation; and I made a vow
to meself against it, for the time was coming,
that young as I was, I might be wanted for
other work; and sure enough the rising came
through the counthry like a flash of lightning,
and of coorse I was soon off and in it. The
masther was in it, too—for it was thick about us
—but not on our side. Well! the enemy was
too much for us. We fought as hard as we
could, and would have marched to glory, if
we had good commanders. Any way, the
short and the long of it was, I was taken
prisoner—small chance I had then. They
used to string us up like herrings on a stick;
turn off a dozen at a time: no' hour for confession—only off you go! I felt mighty
young to be laving the world like that; and
I heard an officer say, it's a shame to hang.

such a boy, or we don't make war against boys—I forget which it was; it was such a word as that. Another said, 'His arm is powerless;' and that put me up to ax for Masther Arthur; but they wouldn't listen, though I prayed to them stronger than ever I prayed to God—more shame for me, only life is sweet! I thought, when I saw what they war doing, that the dead were happy; and I began to think of where I was going, and no one there to say a word for my soul— no priest near me! I thought of the saints and holy martyrs; but still I longed for life. And some were crying, and some took wonderful to the prayers; and the soldiers kept the people off with the points of their bayonets; and anything did for a gallows : but the end of it was, they *hung us*—fifteen at once—and none, not one, three-and-twenty—young, soft, innocent boys! "

"Hung you, Jerry!"

"Aye, bedad; never axed my lave."

" Hung you!"

" Troth, aye, lady dear; and thought no
more about it than if I had been a rat—hung
me! When they hung our leaders they called
it for high treason—when they hung us they
called it for rebellion; but it made no differ—
it was hanging all the same, and in double
quick time too.   I was hung by the neck for
rebellion, as sure as my name is Jerry Swift!
When we war' strung up, the ullagaun that
was raised—the screams and the distraction—
the wildness of the poor helpless women who
saw from the distance all they loved best in
the world tossing in the air, like scarecrows
over a field of young corn, was what I never
heerd but once, and never shall hear again—
oh, those howls and wails! as if all the ban-
shees in Ireland rose from the graves of the
fine ould families, to cry their last cry upon
earth; and, still, above them all I heerd my
mother's keen—she was the finest keener in
all the country—and I thought the sound

filled the heavens; that was the last thought I
had—the very last sound I heard; and the
next—but I must tell you the rights of it: my
little sister (I had but one) had the sense to seek
the masther—it was mighty daring for a slip of
a child, not more than twelve, and small of
her age, to think of it; if she had been oulder,
she would have been afeard of those terrible
men, but she had only me in her thoughts;
she flew through and among the soldiers
calling for Mr. Arthur, just like one mad;
and they stood out of her way, and let her
pass on, like the wind; not one had the heart to
touch her, except in kindness—and God bless
the hand that did so! to this day I pray for it,
and would, though it was red with my own
blood. She was marked for early death,—
and had the look of an angel in her little white
face. She never knew how—but she found
the masther; and, clinging out of his coat, she
tould him how I was cast for a rebel, and
going to be hung; and, without another word,

he seated my little sister on his shoulder, and
away with him through the soldiers and the
people—he did not let the grass grow under
his feet, nor the sun shine in his eyes—he
went, like the wind, until he came upon the
hasty gallows-trees, on which we were string-
ing up, and my poor little sister kept screaming
out, 'Too late, too late;' but the masther,
ma'am, dear, whom you only knew as a quiet,
elderly gentleman, was dauntless and brave
as a lion then; he had no time to go to head-
quarters, or anything, he had only power to
unsling his sword in the face of the whole of
them and cut me down   They said it was a
wonderful sight; the military could no more
understand what he was after than I could
feel it. Why an officer should care for a poor,
miserable rebel, was beyond all thought, and
they stood still, as if themselves war' all dead
men; then the Irish rose a cry, and entreated
the masther, now his hand was in, to go on with
it, and cut down all the poor fellows at onct;

but, of course, he never heeded—only raised me in his arms and carried me to where some of the poor craychurs were screaming and crying about their people. It wasn't needed for him to tell my mother to take me away; they war'ready enough to do that or anything; though it was nothing but a corpse I was, still, they had me safe among them. And the last sight they had of the poor masther, was seeing him turn to some officer, and deliver up his soord.

" It was a foolish thought that came into my head, when I was coming to myself, that I could not understand. I thought purgatory was mighty like ould Ireland, and wondered how my mother got there before me. I was fairly destroyed when I heerd what the master had done, and though I knew his own regiment was in the Indees, and he on lave, yet, I feared they'd make his life answer for mine. But my poor mother, who was a respectable, responsible woman, for a poor woman, said that they would consider *his* life, worth forty of

mine; and that any way I *was* hanged. And
the schoolmaster said, it made all the odds, he
had *not* rescued a prisoner, he had only cut
down a dead body. ' And as he's one of themselves, they'll take it asy,' he says. If I had
been able to stand, I was so distressed
about my noble master, that I would have gone
back, and on my two bare knees, entreated
them to hang me over agen; but I couldn't
move hand or foot; I was as wake as an
infant. My mother tried to get spaking with
Madame Butler. And every boy in the
counthry, that wasn't kilt right off, was book-
swore to save the young masther, if they
offered to touch him. And sure enough, he
had to fly for it, *for my sake*—think of that!
King, Lords and Commons, couldn't have
saved him, for going agen the law, at
such a time, making such an example of
himself and me, before all the people. If he
hadn't had the blood of the Butlers in him,
he'd have been shot, in the strength of the

law, by sunrise the next morning—only think
of that! but the general couldn't say
aginst the ould lady in one way; he didn't
seem to mind what part of the ould place Mr.
Arthur was put up in, so that he was put up,
—and the poor masther was imprisoned in a
room hanging over the river; it was understood at onct, and the boys got a cob-
ble under the window that night, while
the moon was shining on the back of
the clouds — first and foremost was the
boy that took the shot at him and hit my
shoulder, 'deed yes! and he proposed to the
masther to be their leader—the captain over
them all ; and that if he would, we'd be sure
to win Ireland ; but the poor masther had
enough of the wars, and no mind to turn agin'
his own lawful king ; so he just went his way
abroad for a while, and the least thing I could
do, was to follow him, and offer to be his slave
for life ; and I edicated meeself for his sake,
and studied foreign languages, so that at one

time I could '*parley voo*' with any of them,
and what I couldn't say I could do; and we
had a bright time of it. Oh, wasn't it wonderful what that gentleman did for me!"

"And you for him, Jerry."

"Oh, God bless yer honour for thinking of
that, which I don't! sure I was born in the
place; and though he only came in the female
line, and Madame Butler was so angry with
him for what he had done for the likes of me,
—yet he had a right to my life, though I had
none to his."

"Jerry, you did not think of *that* when you
became a united Irishman."

"Oh yes, I did. We never riz agin the
raal ancient ould gentry—only agin the
interlopers. Sure, not one of us that wouldn't
shed our blood as ready as wather for the breed
of the Butlers."

"Yet, one 'boy,' as you call him, would
have shot your master."

"Ah, you see, he went soldiering—took

arums against his country—but look what he
did afther."

" But if his shot had told ?"

" But it didn't," retorted poor Jerry, irrita-
bly, for him, " sure if it had, it's not there he'd
be, now," he looked in at his charge.   " No,
bedad, its not there he'd be now, sleeping like
a new-born babby, with a smile upon his face,
just as if angels war whispering him, and who
can say they are not ?"

He fidgeted about a little, but his strange
story impressed itself so deeply upon me, that
I remained silent.

" Ma'am, dear," he exclaimed, suddenly,
" maybe it's thinking I'm romancing, you are,
but if you'll just be plased to look here, there's
the black mark I shall carry to my grave."

He fell on his knees at my feet, and bent
his great, grizzled, bullet head forward—and
there truly was the livid mark round his
throat.

" There, it's no romance, is it ?   Glory be
to God !"

" One word more, Jerry ; your little sister !"

" Oh, before the month was out, Father
Mulcahey says to me :—'Jerry,' says he,
' ye're happy born ; don't fret,' he says (he
was such a fine, portly man, with enough sunshine in his face to turn night into day, any
time) 'don't fret, nor trouble yerself about
purgatory—I want nothing; for if ever there
was an angel in heaven, ye'r sister's one
already, and there's not a blade of grass
on her grave yet.'"

END OF VOL. II.

CHARLES BEVAN AND SON, PRINTERS, CHAPEL STREET, GROSVENOR SQUARE.

Printed in the United States
149938LV00008B/1/A